CHRISTIANITY AND THE
NATURE OF HISTORY

CHRISTIANITY AND THE NATURE OF HISTORY

BY

H. G. WOOD

HULSEAN LECTURES
1933–1934

CAMBRIDGE
AT THE UNIVERSITY PRESS
1934

CAMBRIDGE
UNIVERSITY PRESS

University Printing House, Cambridge CB2 8BS, United Kingdom

Cambridge University Press is part of the University of Cambridge.

It furthers the University's mission by disseminating knowledge in the pursuit of
education, learning and research at the highest international levels of excellence.

www.cambridge.org
Information on this title: www.cambridge.org/9781107497788

© Cambridge University Press 1934

First published 1934
First paperback edition 2015

A catalogue record for this publication is available from the British Library

ISBN 978-1-107-49778-8 Paperback

DEDICATED

TO

THE MASTER AND FELLOWS

OF

JESUS COLLEGE

CAMBRIDGE

Contents

A Preface

IN offering to a wider public the Hulsean Lectures delivered in the Divinity School at Cambridge during the Autumn Term of 1933, I must express my deep and abiding gratitude to the electors for giving me this privilege and this opportunity. I count it a high privilege to be allowed to stand in a succession which includes the names of so many to whom I look up as teachers and fathers in God. I count it also a high privilege to be asked to follow Dr Anderson Scott, the first Free Churchman among my predecessors. It is no small gratification to realise that I am the first member of the Society of Friends, and also the first layman, to hold the position of Hulsean lecturer. However inadequately one may discharge the duties of the office, to have held it, and to have enjoyed thereby renewed contact with the life of the University, is an enrichment of experience and memory for which one cannot be too thankful.

My sense of indebtedness to the electors is enhanced by the opportunity they have given me of formulating certain convictions concerning Christianity and history which have long been with me and which are to me of fundamental importance.

It may not be out of place to say something in this preface of the influences which have shaped and determined the growth of these convictions in my mind. No one can fully analyse himself or trace exactly the sources of his working faith, but to indicate the factors, personal and literary, of whose influence he is aware, enables readers to appreciate or discount more easily the positions for which he is contending. Under modern conditions, to write the history of one's religious opinions ceases to be an exercise in vanity and becomes an obligation of sincerity due to one's critics, whether friendly or hostile.

In discussing the interpretation of Christianity as an historic faith, I hope to do justice to my Free Church inheritance, to my upbringing among the Baptists, and to the insight which I owe to membership in the Society of Friends, but I cannot and do not approach the theme from any strictly denominational angle. In the influence of my home there was present already a blending of the Anglican and the Free Church traditions, for while my father was a Baptist minister, my mother was the daughter of a clergyman of the Church of Ireland. She died while I was still in 'the small years' and before she could exert a direct influence on my intellectual development in the narrower sense of the term; but seated by her in the family pew in chapel, I learned habits and attitudes of devotion which were perhaps more characteristic of the Church of England than of the Free Churches. She taught me to pray, and from her I learned the great confirmation hymn, "O Jesus, I have promised to serve Thee to the end". She instilled into me the reverence for Jesus which continues to be the centre of my faith. If the critics, having read so far, now dismiss my religious outlook as the product of a mother-fixation, I should be ashamed to deny the facts which give colour to such a suggestion. But I have not found that lessons learned at one's mother's knee are necessarily to be discarded in the light of later experience.

The influence of my father was exerted over a much longer period and was more varied in character. He exemplified what Mackail in his life of William Morris calls the "steady and almost stolid dutifulness" of the mid-Victorian middle-class, particularly of the mid-Victorian Nonconformist. My father put his work first, and as he was a Baptist minister, much of his work centred in his study. Consequently the organisation of the life of the home was largely determined by the requirements of his calling. Without any insistence or formal teaching on his part, my father's example made an ideal of a life dedicated to duty seem natural to his children. A generation emancipated by Lytton Strachey has learned to discount this mid-Victorian sense of duty. Looking back, I realise certain limitations in it. My father was undoubtedly limited on the side of recreation, and he was usually glad to get back from any holiday he took. But I do not see that the post-war generation can really face its tasks without a sense of duty. The anti-Puritan is likely to fall victim to the coarse external disciplines of Communist or Fascist dictatorships, if he refuses the necessity of self-discipline. I count it a gain to have grown up in an atmosphere where the ideas of vocation and of diligence in one's vocation were taken for granted.

In family worship and in Saturday evening Bible lessons, my father taught us to know and reverence the Bible. He regarded the Bible as the record of a unique revelation, and in relation to critical inquiries he was cautious to the verge of conservatism. But he never linked appreciation of the Bible with reverence for the letter. He was satisfied with Bishop Westcott's doctrine of plenary inspiration, and though he was a friend and admirer of C. H. Spurgeon, he could not follow the great preacher in the once-famous 'down-grade' controversy among the Baptists. My father was not prepared to make "the verbal inspiration and inerrancy of the Scriptures" an essential article of faith, or to exclude from the Baptist ministry those who could not accept this doctrine. For myself, it meant that I never had painfully to unlearn a theory of inspiration which is incompatible with modern knowledge, and I could accept the methods and results of historical and literary criticism without feeling that faith was endangered.

The fellowship of the Baptist church in Upper Holloway, where my father ministered for over thirty years, was a primary factor in mediating historic Christianity to me. Attendance at Sunday School and Bible Class had incidentally the effect of quickening my sympathy with folk of varied social standing. The church really effected an intermingling of classes, and exhibited Christ's power to bridge social gulfs. One secret of the church life was my father's pastoral gift. He would pay on an average twenty-three or twenty-four visits a week. Thus in practice was demonstrated the Christian valuation of the individual, a valuation which is likewise safeguarded among the Baptists by their characteristic insistence on personal decision. Membership in such a church meant that one grew into certain Christian attitudes of mind almost without being aware of it.

Naturally, as I advanced in years, my father's library and my father's advice about reading played an important part in the development of my knowledge and thought, especially on the subject of religion. My father would often draw my attention to books which he could not unreservedly commend. Thus he advised me to read Farrar's *Eternal Hope*, a book which set me free from the tyranny and torment of belief in eternal punishment. My father himself, though attracted to Farrar's position, did not accept or preach it, because he thought Farrar did not treat the Scripture evidence fairly. In the same way, he was interested in the doctrine of conditional immortality advocated by Edward White and Dr Agar Beet, but while there was much to be said for it, he was not convinced that it represented Scripture teaching on this theme. The balance of scriptural evidence seemed to favour the traditional teaching on eternal punishment. And if it be assumed, as was then commonly assumed, that there must be in the Bible one consistent doctrine on this subject, I think my father was right in his reserves. Neither Farrar nor Edward White could fairly establish his claim to be giving the full sense of the Scriptures. The case is altered, if we are presented with tendencies of thought within the pages of the Bible which are not completely harmonised and which we have to evaluate afresh. But it was characteristic of my father that he encouraged me to read Farrar, while himself entertaining such reserves on

Farrar's teaching. In the same spirit he drew my attention to Herrmann's golden book, *The Christian's Communion with God*. To my father, Herrmann appeared to be a rather confused and woolly writer, and the Ritschlian distinction between fact and value seemed to suggest a dangerous double standard of truth. But he suspected that Herrmann might have something to say to me, and he was not mistaken. I have since those days realised the danger of divorcing judgments of value from judgments of existence, and I cannot isolate the fact of Christ as Herrmann does in his polemic against mysticism. But Herrmann made clear to me the difference between accepting an orthodox creed and truly seeing God in Jesus. I perceived that one might have a correct theology without possessing true religion. The same lesson had come home to me in reading Stopford Brooke's life of F. W. Robertson of Brighton, particularly in reading Robertson's tremendous replies to his Evangelical critics. I could see that one might be firm as 'The Rock' and yet be a stranger to the spirit of Jesus. At the same time Herrmann deepened my conviction that what lies behind the orthodox creeds is vital Christianity, that Jesus saves us by showing us not what man may be but what God is, that He is only leader and example because He is Lord, that a humanist interpretation of Christ can never save mankind. Herrmann impressed on my mind the unique significance of the revelation of God through this historic person, Jesus.

Perhaps the most far-reaching single suggestion in regard to books which I owed to my father came through his offer of half-a-crown to me in my 'teens, if I would read through Butler's *Analogy* during a summer holiday. I gained much more than half-a-crown from accepting the challenge. I read the famous apologetic in a compact and rather forbidding edition which Dr Angus had prepared for his students at Regent's Park College. The edition is enriched with a careful analysis and some judicious notes. Certain impressions were left on my mind which have deepened with the years. No one can read the *Analogy* without realising that the Christian thinker is at once more profound and more conscientious than the Deist writers whose position he is examining. He is more scrupulously fair to them than they ever tried to be to traditional Christianity. He is facing reality and is open to truth in a manner not exemplified by his rationalist opponents. Toland, Collins and the rest of them are shallow in comparison with Bishop Butler. The first four books of Hooker's *Ecclesiastical Polity* make a somewhat similar impression. However much Hooker was

hampered in the later books, especially in the
posthumous books, by his resolve to defend a somewhat arbitrary *status quo* in church order and administration, in his grasp of principles he has out-
stripped Thomas Cartwright and the Elizabethan
Puritans. But to return to Butler, acquaintance
with the *Analogy* created a presumption in my
mind against humanism and rationalism. I expected to find that writers and thinkers who maintain the traditions of Renaissance humanism and
eighteenth-century rationalism would be clever
rather than wise, frank and outspoken rather than
responsible and conscientious, stimulating by the
freshness and wittiness of their observations rather
than impressive by the weight of their judgments.
And so far my expectation has been constantly
realised. The genuine Christian thinkers are still
in my judgment out-thinking the best representa-
tives of the rationalist tradition.

I must briefly allude to three other impressions
that remained after reading Butler. We no longer
conceive the relations of natural and revealed
religion exactly as the eighteenth-century thinkers
conceived them, but the inadequacy of any form
of natural religion remains manifest. Even within
the framework of the distinction he accepted,
Butler convinced me that God must meet us and
has met us in history, that God is to be understood

through a revelation in history and not simply or
chiefly through the order of nature. I did not of
course fully understand this as a boy, but Butler
put me on my guard against specious claims for
natural religion and natural theology. Similarly,
I did not at once see the full force of the bishop's
insistence on probability as the guide of life. But
two applications of the principle have gradually
become clear to me. The first is that no ultimate
belief is likely to be free from difficulties and objections, and that the difficulties and objections
attaching to different ultimate beliefs must be
honestly compared. The rationalist answer to
Butler is to abandon Deism. If Butler shows the
same or similar difficulties inherent in natural
religion as are alleged by Deists to characterise
revealed religion, then let us surrender natural
religion along with revelation. But clearly Butler's
method can be carried further. If the rationalist
abandons Deism to escape Butler, he must take
refuge in some form of materialism or scepticism,
and the difficulties, intellectual and moral, of such
positions can be shown to be more serious than
those of Deism itself. When, at the University, the
difficulties of Christian theism were forced on my
attention, I did not feel inclined hastily to throw
over theism, because I knew that the difficulties of
other positions might prove more serious than

those I was asked to recognise in theism. The second application of Butler's principle concerns the weight to be given to history in one's ultimate beliefs. Since historical evidence is always in some degree doubtful, many would ignore history altogether. But if we may not neglect probabilities, such ignoring of history is unjustifiable, and borders on intellectual dishonesty.

It is relevant to my purpose to recall one more debt to my father. He fostered my interest in general history. For many years in the summer season at least I used to read standard histories to him for half an hour before breakfast, and, in that way, we read together the major works of Macaulay and Froude. I must also have read Motley and J. R. Green about the same period, whether to myself or aloud to my father. No doubt I then acquired a Whig and Protestant bias. My Nonconformist upbringing, however, saved me from succumbing to Froude's Erastianism, and among the passages which stand out in my memory most vividly are his account of the martyrdom of blessed John Fisher, and his reference to a group of nameless Anabaptists from Holland who were also executed in the time of Henry VIII, and who thus helped "to pay the price of English freedom". Hatred of religious intolerance became second nature to me.

Some of the English classics prescribed for the sixth form at the City of London School left their mark on my mind. I entered the school after Dr Abbott had resigned the headmastership, but I suspect that Bacon's *Essays* and Milton's *Areopagitica* were texts which he had chosen and which his successor wisely continued. Milton in particular appealed to me, and his tract in defence of liberty of the press at least saved me from the folly of supposing that the great liberties, the liberty of speech and public meeting, the liberty of inquiry and of publication, the liberty of worship and of prophesying, were mere embellishments of the desire of the rising bourgeois class to make money unrestrained by King or Archbishop or Court of High Commission. Having read Milton, I shall never be taken in by Mr John Strachey or Mr Hilaire Belloc.

While Milton confirmed my love of liberty as an essential of the good life, Burke's *Reflections on the French Revolution*, which I also read at school, taught me the value of historical continuity. I fell under the spell of Burke as I had previously fallen under the spell of Milton, and I found no incompatibility in my enthusiasms. Along with Burke I read de Tocqueville on the ancient *régime* in France. The combined effect of Burke and de Tocqueville was to implant in my mind a distrust of violent revolutionaries as the victims of romantic illusions—a distrust which recent events alike in Russia and in Germany have served only to deepen.

It is to the University that I owe my fuller introduction to the study of history. I do not remember indeed to have received much formal instruction in the methods of historical inquiry. At some time or other I came across Seignobos' admirable little volume, and when I was preparing to take up the work of History tutor at Jesus College, G. T. Lapsley drew my attention to the massive tome of Bernheim. But the foundations of historical judgment were laid for me by reading for the Classical Tripos, at first under Arthur Gray, the present Master of the College, and later under Edwin Abbott. To their careful tuition, to their literary judgment and exact scholarship, I owe such rudiments of the intellectual discipline needed for historical inquiries as I was capable of absorbing. It is hardly necessary to recall how the essentials of an historian's equipment are bound up with a classical training. To translate any classical text, one must discipline one's self to discover what the author himself meant to say and not what one would wish or expect him to say. The successful solution of the problem of translation presupposes acquaintance

with the distinctive genius of two languages and
so requires a sense of historical perspective. The
classical scholar is constantly engaged in the art
of comparison. He is always studying parallels
and learning both to recognise true similarities,
and to discern real differences behind superficial
resemblances. The main essentials of an honest
interpretation of historical documents are thus
conveyed through the study of the classics.

The elements of textual criticism with which I
first became acquainted in the classical school,
I was to study more exhaustively in reading for
the Theological Tripos. The fascinating problems
of the editing of the text of the New Testament,
still unsolved, partly through the very wealth of
material at our disposal, form incomparably the
finest training-ground for the textual critic. Here
Hort's masterly introduction remains the indispensable guide to true scholarship; not that the
student will be slavishly bound to Hort's conclusions, but that he must understand Hort's principles
and methods, and must drink deep of his scientific
spirit. I had the good fortune to enter upon this
particular study when Rendel Harris was still
Reader in Ancient Palaeography. Himself Hort's
pupil, he combined reverence for Hort's memory
with an inclination to question every one of Hort's
judgments. I learned from Rendel Harris to

temper respect for the conservative maxim, "The more difficult reading is to be preferred", with confidence in the daring assertion that "nothing is so certain as a good conjecture". I also learned that genius knows no rules, but immediately the more important lesson was the discovery of the interest and independence of what is usually termed lower or textual criticism. I realised how worthless all historical constructions must necessarily be, if they are not based on a careful editing of texts and an accurate weighing of authorities.

Along with the teaching of Rendel Harris, I regard the tuition of F. J. Foakes-Jackson, the lectures of H. M. Gwatkin, and the writings of T. R. Glover as among the more important influences determining my understanding of the history of Christianity. W. K. L. Clarke in the dedication of his *New Testament Problems* has characterised so admirably the informality of Foakes-Jackson's converse with his students, that I need not say more here about his methods. But I shall never forget the value of the special coaching he gave me when I was reading for the Lightfoot. He combined a sense of the relative importance of different events, movements, and tendencies, with an interest in often trivial but piquant detail. To read under his guidance was to begin to appreciate the true standards of historical significance. As for Gwatkin's lectures, I suppose it would be difficult to count the students who first learned in his lecture-room the real meaning of history and historical study. Perhaps the great value of his course on early church history lay not so much in the stimulus of his Tacitean epigrams, nor yet in the independence and breadth of his judgments, but in his insistence on treating the history of the Christian church as enmeshed in the warp and woof of general European history. He was a great church historian precisely because his interests were not narrowly ecclesiastic. The qualities of Glover's work are well known. I still remember hearing him speak to a rowdy street-boys' club in Cambridge on the boyhood of Jesus— an address which is now embodied substantially in the opening chapter of the *Jesus of History*, and which was, unless I am much mistaken, the actual germ of that now famous book. It exemplified Glover's interest in local colour, his power of recreating an historical background. But more important is his conviction manifest in every book, that the interest of history centres in persons and personal character, and most enviable is his power of etching in a portrait in a succession of short sharp isolated strokes, as in his masterly chapters on Tertullian and Clement of Alexandria, in *The Conflict of Religions*. When I am wearied with the efforts of Marxists and others to torture the realities of history to fit their dogmatic formulae, I turn with relief to Glover, to regain my sanity and my humanity.

If these were among the more positive influences which shaped my intellectual development, I owe almost as much to those who forced me to dissent from some of their characteristic attitudes. Undoubtedly, two of the most influential and attractive thinkers and teachers in the University in my undergraduate days were G. Lowes Dickinson and J. McT. E. McTaggart. Both attracted and influenced me, and the influence was not merely negative, though both drove me to conclusions different from their own. My first personal contact with Lowes Dickinson came through my being able to give him some trifling assistance in an inquiry into the hours of work and the remuneration of college bedmakers. The example as well as the writings of this gentle humanist helped to quicken my response to the claims of social justice. In other directions too he challenged one's imperfect sympathies and one's insensitiveness to beauty in nature and in art. But when I came to read his little book, *Religion: a criticism and a forecast,* which made a considerable stir in the University at the time, I found I could not accept its main thesis. Lowes Dickinson contrasted religion with science, faith with knowledge. The realm of the unknown belongs to religion and faith; the realm of the known belongs to science. Faith is conceived as pioneering for knowledge. The religious imagination, groping about in the unknown, produces helpful mythologies for science to test. Religious faith, if it is honest, holds a dagger to its breast, and awaits the signal from science whether to press the dagger home or breathe again. Such a thesis rests upon Comte's view of religion, or rather of theology as primitive science, destined to be replaced by science proper, or else upon Herbert Spencer's doctrine of the unknown or unknowable as the true sphere of religion. To me this whole view of religion seemed then and seems now fundamentally mistaken. Religious faith is not framing hypotheses to guide the inquiries of natural scientists. The religious-minded man is not seeking the same kind of explanation of the world as the scientist. The religious interpretation of the universe is no substitute for a natural scientific interpretation, nor can the latter ever take the place of the former. Religious faith is concerned as much with the known as with the unknown. It cannot be confined to the field not yet occupied by science. The passage from faith to knowledge, from hope to sight, is not a passage from religion to science.

The knowledge and vision at which we arrive are as definitely religious as the faith and hope from which we set out. Religion is not moving in a realm of guess-work. It has its own records of achievements and discoveries. It can point to the verification and clarification of faith's hypotheses in actual experience. I found myself once again affirming that the evidence for the truth of religion in general and of Christianity in particular must be found in history.

Just at this point, my dissent from Lowes Dickinson intensified. For in his little book, he committed himself to two positions disallowing the appeal to history. He maintained first that the ideal embodied in Christ's story should have just the same influence upon us whether the story be fact or fiction, and second that the evidence is so doubtful, the creation of fictitious personalities so easy, that a rational man will seek elsewhere than in history the basis of his belief and conduct. Both these positions seemed to me definitely untenable. The first is an academic fallacy. An ideal realised in actual life has more claim upon our attention and our loyalty than an ideal presented in the form of fiction. Biographies do actually and rightly weigh more with us than romances. As to the difficulties and uncertainties of historical evidence, they form no justification for ignoring historical probabilities. Lowes Dickinson omitted to point out the alternative undisputed certainties on which we are to base our belief and conduct. There are no such bases for our faith, and the only certainty resulting from this deliberate disregard of history will be the vitiating of our philosophy by adopting an inadequate basis. Our belief and conduct will both be wrong if we refuse to take into account the probabilities established by historical inquiry.

Like many others, I found a great stimulus in Dr McTaggart's popular course on metaphysics without tears, or philosophy for non-professionals. His confidence in reason and in reasoning, the clarity, the subtlety and the courage of his argumentation, the boldness and the independence of his speculative theories, were alike a challenge and an inspiration. Incidentally, he exposed to my satisfaction the fallacies of materialism, and he also confirmed my distrust of restrictions on intellectual inquiry. Yet so far as I could grasp it, his own philosophical position did not convince me. I felt rather than thought that the basis of experience on which his philosophy rested was too narrow to sustain the superstructure. The one issue on which I ventured to cross swords with him while I was a junior don was the worth of the appeal of Augustine and Pascal to man's restless longing after God. McTaggart dismissed the argument of "Thou wouldst not be seeking Me, if thou hadst not already found Me", by asserting the general principle, "Nothing is true merely because we wish it to be true". That principle seemed to me sound and yet quite inconclusive, if not irrelevant, as regards the point under discussion. When the Psalmist writes of the thirst of his soul after the living God, he is not assuming some theory of the universe to be true, because he wishes it to be true. Such a deep-seated longing is as strong a proof of the reality of God as some extravagance in the movement of an observed planet is evidence of the pull of some planet unseen. A modern writer has pointed out that if a man is genuinely converted, he is converted not to theism but to God. This very essential difference McTaggart never seemed to me fully to appreciate. I could neither follow nor refute his subtle arguments for the unreality of Time, but I did not believe in his conclusions. If Hegelian dialectic implied that Time is not real and that history has no abiding interest, then I was convinced and I remain convinced that there is something wrong with Hegelian dialectic.

More and more I tended to take a writer's valuation of history and his appreciation of the methods of historical science as the criterion of the worth of his philosophy. In particular this became

my test of all works representative of militant
rationalism. Haeckel's *Riddle of the Universe* and
Blatchford's *God and my Neighbour* were vigorously
discussed about the time I graduated. I found it
difficult to believe in Haeckel's reputation as a
scientist when I discovered his uncritical gullibility
in the realm of Church History. I have since
realised that natural scientists who will be strictly
loyal to scientific standards in their own laboratories may be quite unaware of the existence of
such standards in the realm of historical research.
Blatchford put forward views about the trust-
worthiness of the text of the New Testament, and
the value of the gospels as historical documents,
which have indeed played a considerable part in
rationalist propaganda but which have no place
in scientific criticism. That he could invoke in
support of such views the great name of T. H.
Huxley shook my faith not in the gospels but in
Huxley. Nor was I more favourably impressed
by Mr Philip Vivian's *The Churches and Modern
Thought*, which by the kindness of some supporter
of the Rationalist Press Association was circulated
freely to University students when it appeared in
a cheap edition. The book is well adapted to
appeal to the half-educated. Modern thought, as
Mr Vivian interprets it, is concerned not so much
to discover the truth about Christianity, as to find

excuses for a lazy scepticism. His style of argument is parallel to the rationalist appeal to the one hundred and fifty-seven sects in *Whitaker's Almanack*. The Fundamentalists and Bishop Gore disagree. What then is the poor man in the street to believe? Divergences among critics are manifold. The problem of Christian origins is obscure and perhaps insoluble. The most likely solution is that which is most remote from traditional orthodoxy. It may be that Jesus never existed, and in any case Christianity is an artificial synthesis of previously existing factors with no distinctive quality or living spirit of its own. That is the gist of Mr Vivian's contention, and it constitutes a stern indictment of modern thought. Any one who has ever come near the living heart of Christianity will be unmoved by it. I once handed Vivian's book to an Armenian Christian who had been through the fires of persecution and had discovered therein the meaning of his faith. When he gave it back to me, he said quite simply, "I did not know before that it was so hard to write against religion". But to any one who wishes to set Christianity on one side and to feel enlightened and up-to-date in so doing, Mr Vivian's book will make an immediate appeal. To me the great lesson of the book was the discovery that rationalism and love of truth are not exact equivalents.

I do not remember when my friend C. K. Ogden organised the Heretics, dedicated to the great principle of not believing anything except upon evidence. Fidelity to this principle was displayed in taking seriously any theory however unsubstantial and fantastic so long as it was unorthodox. Ogden himself at that time practised a somewhat indiscriminate intellectual charity, which has since produced splendid fruit in the Library of Philosophy and Psychology. He hospitably entertained strangers who did not always turn out to be angels, but he nursed the hope that the latest heretical goose would prove a philosophic swan. Through Ogden and the Heretics I became interested in the Christ-myth controversy. Two features of the work of Arthur Drews arrested my attention. In the first place it was clear that his historical judgments were determined by his philosophy and not by a straightforward survey of the evidence. To his type of spiritual monism a faith which attaches value to historic events or persons is a kind of idolatry. I failed to see why the question of the historicity of Jesus should be determined in defiance of the principles of rational criticism, merely to bolster up the philosophic prejudices of Arthur Drews. In the second place, I perceived that the substance of his arguments was drawn from the writings of Mr J. M. Robertson. The real case was to be found in *Pagan Christs* and *Christianity and Mythology*. In these primary sources I studied it, and satisfied myself that Mr Robertson's theories, though presented with amazing ingenuity and learning, were yet definitely unscientific. In the last analysis, the whole Christ-myth theorising is a glaring example of obscurantism, if the sin of obscurantism consists in the acceptance of bare possibilities in place of actual probabilities, and of pure surmise in defiance of existing evidence. Those who have not entered far into the laborious inquiry may pretend that the historicity of Jesus is an open question. For me to adopt such a pretence would be sheer intellectual dishonesty. I know I must, as an honest man, reckon with Jesus as a factor in history. I cannot rightly ignore or evade the challenge of His story. I am not ashamed to embrace the hopes which that story inspires.

Through Rendel Harris in the first instance I was brought into contact with the Society of Friends. At his invitation I went to Woodbrooke, and since 1910 have been co-operating with Friends in that educational experiment. In 1923, I was admitted to membership in the Society. The influence of Quakerism helped to save me from sheer historicism. I do not know that I was ever tempted to regard the Jesus of history as "a dead fact stranded on the shore of the oblivious years", but I was in some danger of being preoccupied with Jesus as a figure in history and so of failing to hear the Lord Himself say, "Arise, let us go hence". I was a Marcan rather than a Johannine Christian. And while the Synoptic portraits of Jesus mean not less but rather more than before, and while they continue to be, in Glover's phrase, "anchors in the actual", which check misdirected flights of mystical fancy that claim to represent the eternal Christ, yet the fourth evangelist's interpretation of the Christ eternal and his doctrine of the Paraclete, the spirit of truth, seem to me now the charter of Christian liberty and progress. Friends help me to believe more courageously in the "contemporary inspiration of the Holy Spirit", to realise that Jesus Christ is Himself the 'moving subject' of history, and that the Christian faith is not historical simply in the sense that it is dependent on past events and their significance, but also in the sense that it is creative and determinative of the history that has yet to be made. The triumphs of Christianity lie ahead of us.

To speak of the prospective triumphs of Christianity may seem a mockery at a time when we are so far from having repaired the moral losses of the war and when there are so many signs of a return to the Dark Ages in Europe. But manifestly, "it is now that Christ needs us, if ever He did". And to me it seems that we cannot offer Christ to-day the service He requires of us, unless we realise the incompatibility of war with the spirit of Christianity. The weapons of our warfare are not and cannot be carnal. Yet Friends' testimony against war, though it be a valid interpretation of the gospel, will not be effective as an isolated negation. Its validity is dependent on the positive valuation of human personality which is bound up with the gospel. Friends, in my judgment, have understood rightly some of the great implications of the Christian estimate of the worth of the human soul. This Christian valuation commits us in theory and in practice to the spiritual equality of the sexes, to a profound reverence for childhood, to the constant reliance on persuasion and co-operation, to the resolve to labour for the removal of oppression without ever resorting to the oppressors' weapons. I am persuaded that only in loyalty to these fundamentals can we serve Christ to-day.

It is indeed, as I see it, a weakness among some modern Friends that they are content to ground their principles and their practice on some rather vague interpretations of the divine seed in every man, interpretations which tend to shade off into humanism or pantheism and which permit Friends to sit loose to historic Christianity. The Quaker doctrine of the inward light is many-sided, and in all its possible meanings is suggestive and helpful, but its very ambiguities put a premium on hazy thinking and incline some to mistake the presuppositions or the corollaries of the gospel for the gospel itself. For me at least the spirit of Christianity which I believe Friends have rightly understood is derived from and dependent on the character of the historical incarnation. It is because God sent His Son in mercy and not in wrath, to draw men not to drive them, to persuade and not to compel, it is because violence belongeth not to God, that we must endeavour to live in the spirit that sees to the end of all wars. Beloved, if it was thus that God loved us, we must also in the same manner love one another. In this spirit we must fashion history.

*   *   *   *   *

For the general view of the nature of history, expressed or implied in these lectures, I am deeply indebted to the writings of Ernst Troeltsch, particularly to volume III of his collected works, *Der Historismus und seine Probleme*, and to the earlier short course on *Moderne Geschichtsphilosophie* included in volume II. I shall count myself happy if I succeed in making some of his positions clear to English readers. Of fundamental importance is the distinction drawn by Windelband and Rickert, and developed by Troeltsch, between two types of science, the nomothetic and the idiographic, the one concerned with the discovery of fruitful general principles, the other with the appreciation of particulars whose nature cannot be fully explained by general laws; the one interested in particular facts for the sake of discovering general laws, the other interested in general laws for the sake of appreciating individuality and value; the one concerned with the phenomena of repetition, the other with the unique and non-repeatable elements of experience: the one best represented by physics, and the other best represented in history. These two types of science are distinct though inseparable. Physics cannot dispense with brute facts, and no advance in the physical sciences can exhaustively explain the detail of the universe; history can get nowhere as the science of the individual if it does not accept and exploit generalisations to the full. But Henri Berr's criticism of this German school seems to me to fail. He treats a valid protest against an artificial and dangerous separation of the sciences as an effective denial of the distinction between them. His own view of history in *La Synthèse* compels him to reaffirm the historian's concern with that which is unique, individual and original. Lest it should be thought that this view of history is peculiarly German, it may be well to remind readers that essentially the same position is worked out independently and forcibly by Benedetto Croce.

This reading of the nature of history and of its character as a science is ignored or misunderstood, wherever the Positivist view of science as knowledge of one type procured by a uniform method is generally accepted. The exponents of scientific humanism in this country still cling to the Positivist conception of science, and are apparently unaware that any revision of this conception is needed. The partial world-views to which they commit themselves and which they proclaim as the outcome of 'science' will only be corrected when we take history seriously, and when we take history seriously we shall find that we cannot regard religion as projection or illusion.

H. G. W.

1934

Lecture I

CHRISTIANITY AND THE NATURE
OF HISTORY

But now *once for all* at the consummation of the ages, He has
been manifested to put away sin through His sacrifice.

HEBREWS IX. 26

For Christ died for sin *once for all*, the just for the sake of the
unjust, to bring us to God.

I PETER III. 18

IN attempting to discharge the duties of the office
which it is my privilege to hold for this year in
the University, I cannot but recall the debt
that I owe to the many influences, intellectual and
personal, which helped to form and clarify my
fundamental convictions during the years I spent
here before the war. Had these lectures been delivered under the old regulations, they would have
been prefaced by the bidding prayer, and I should
have invited you to pray for the University in
general and, as in private duty bound, for the
Master, the Fellows and Scholars of Jesus College,
in particular. I must at least be allowed to prefix
to these lectures this inadequate expression of a
personal indebtedness to the University and to my
college, of which I become more conscious with
the years.

W

I

No one can pass through the University and respond to its influence without acquiring a deeper loyalty to the scientific spirit. We learn here how to value highly accuracy in expression, to distrust what Lord Acton used to call "the slovenly use of the big brush", to pay attention to detail, perhaps to be empirical and realist rather than speculative and idealist. Dr Hort, writing to Edward White Benson on his appointment to Canterbury, spoke of "the danger of the calm and unobtrusive alienation [of the English Church] in thought and spirit from the great silent multitude of Englishmen, and again of alienation from fact and love of fact;—mutual alienations both".[1] Cambridge theology, largely under the influence of Hort himself, has always been apprehensive of this danger, and has contributed much to counteract it. If Cambridge has not produced schools of theology, at least we may claim that in the pursuit of theological studies here men should learn the essentials of the scientific spirit as surely as they do in our natural science laboratories. Perhaps Cambridge may boast that in her study of the humanities she impresses on her sons and daughters the need for accuracy of thought and expression more effectively than she does even through her mathematical and scientific disciplines. It is easily understood that a

[1] *The Life and Letters of F. J. A. Hort*, vol. ii, p. 290.

Chinese philosophical inquirer learned little about the nature of the universe and much about the use of the English language from a visit to Cambridge.[1]

There is indeed some danger of the scientific spirit so conceived issuing in reticence, in suspense of judgment, in confining attention to inquiries where the facts involved are capable of more exact definition and interpretation, and in neglect of the fields where the relevant data are less readily described and comprehended. The old and possibly apocryphal story of the Cambridge classic, whose ambition was to translate Plato rather than to understand him, is a familiar illustration of this tendency. In the same spirit, Cambridge alike in classics and in New Testament studies has shone even more in textual than in higher criticism. It is then with some misgiving that I venture to discuss some of the larger issues in the relation of Christianity to history. I should have been better advised to have devoted my time and yours to some more limited inquiry. Yet there is precedent in earlier Hulsean Lectures for dealing with so large a theme, and it is worth while to direct attention to fundamental questions, however inadequate one's treatment of such questions must inevitably be. As one grows older, one realises the necessity of living in the spirit of that mysterious

[1] *Cambridge University Studies*, p. 30.

sentence from a famous manual of Greek prose, which ran, "I offer myself to be cut and burnt". If we confess our faith, the very poverty of our confession may still help others to get nearer to the truth.

I propose, then, in this course of lectures to examine some important questions involved in the fact that Christianity is definitely an historic faith. I shall ask in the first place whether the emphasis on historic happenings which is characteristic of Christianity is not in line with the nature of history as the modern historian conceives it, and with the whole trend of history as a science in recent years. But if we grant that the Christian valuation of historic events is congenial to the modern historian's outlook, the nature of the actual happenings in which Christianity has its origin is not thereby determined. The prevalence of sociological modes of approach compels us to ask whether the Christian's devotion to the historic person can be justified. In the second lecture therefore I shall consider the relation of great men to social forces in history.

The study of the past inevitably raises the question of providence. Does a divinity really shape our ends, or is the sense which great men and communities have often had, of being the instruments of destiny, a pure illusion? The rise of

Christianity is in some sort a test case. Does the coming of Jesus as and when He did justify, if it does not compel, our faith in God's over-ruling providence? This will be the subject of the third lecture.

In the ebb and flow of the fortunes of men and societies in history, in the rise and fall of kingdoms and institutions, of systems of thought and modes of culture, can we discern the operation of a moral law, or is everything determined by the interplay of non-moral forces, physical or economic? Must we reject or can we reaffirm the prophetic interpretation of history? In lecture four, I shall argue that Christ establishes the prophetic standpoint and gives it its final form and validity.

Amid all the changes and chances of the historic process men have come to believe in the reality of progress. What do we mean by progress? Has progress really occurred? If we can perceive real elements of progress, have we any guarantee of their continued advance? In lecture five, I shall contend that apart from Christ we have no satisfactory standard and no reliable safeguard of progress.

If our confidence in progress be restored, can any vision or hope of a good time coming on this earth satisfy our deepest spiritual needs? Is any form of this-world religion defensible? In the sixth and concluding lecture, I shall submit that true religion must be a religion of eternity as well as a religion of time, and that only in Christianity have we that association of time with eternity, of history with super-history, which is the hall-mark of true religion.

To turn then to our first main topic, it is manifest that the connection of Christianity with history is peculiarly intimate. The Apostles' Creed emphasises, not, as we might expect, the truth of Christ's teaching, but the significance of His birth, death and resurrection. The Christian faith is bound up with certain events and with their historicity. As, I believe, Professor Burkitt has pointed out, in the clauses *conceived by the Holy Ghost, born of the Virgin Mary*, the stress does not fall on the virginity of Mary, but on the assertions that Jesus was truly born as a little child, and was truly divine at and from the moment of His birth. What is denied is Gnostic speculation which fastened on the baptism[1] or the scene in the synagogue at Nazareth as the occasion for the manifestation of the divine Christ in Jesus. Similarly, the phrases *suffered under Pontius Pilate, was crucified, dead and buried* are aimed at all Docetic theories which denied the reality of Christ's sufferings and death. The historicity and significance of these

[1] Such speculations are revived in modern Theosophy and Anthroposophy. Cf. Rudolf Steiner, *Christianity as Mystical Fact*, p. 202.

events were affirmed as essential to the Christian view of God and the world as soon as the content of the faith required to be elaborated beyond the simple confession: 'Jesus is Lord'.

This association of revelation with historic events is characteristic of Judaism and Islam, as well as of Christianity, and it is peculiar to these religions. The great religious systems of the Far East and particularly of India exhibit no such close connection between religion and history. The attraction of primitive Buddhism for many moderns lies in its independence of the figure of its founder and in its aloofness from history as well as in its apparent ignoring of God and immortality. True religious wisdom we are told is to be found in the East, just because Oriental religious philosophies ask us to accept eternal principles rather than to reverence personalities or to affirm the reality of alleged happenings in the past. A typical example of this reaction may be found in a letter of Professor Sir Walter Raleigh written to his sister in 1899. "It seems absurd to subordinate philosophy to certain historical events in Palestine—more and more absurd to me, I think. The *ideas* of Christianity are always interesting: but they are all to be found elsewhere and are not, it would seem, the chief part of its attraction."[1]

[1] *Letters of Sir Walter Raleigh*, p. 209.

Is it then a real weakness in Christianity that it is involved in an entangling alliance with history? Is it a concession, perhaps necessary but certainly dangerous, to the limitations of the man in the street, who cannot grasp general principles in the abstract but must have truth embodied in a tale?

We must either rest in some such judgment as this, or come to realise that the association of Christianity with history is essential gospel, that Christianity is more profoundly true than Hinduism and Buddhism, precisely because historical events mean more to the Christian than they do to the Buddhist or the Hindu. As between Judaism, Christianity and Islam, the crucial issue will turn on whether individual events and the historic process as a whole are more intelligible, more full of meaning from the Christian than from either the Jewish or the Moslem standpoint. To put it in another way, it depends on whether in the course of history Christianity can do fuller justice to Judaism and Islam than Judaism or Islam can do to Christianity.

To me it seems that the affirmations which the modern historian is obliged to make regarding the nature of history and the claims he has to make regarding the independence and importance of his science confirm the emphasis placed on historic events in the Christian faith and may indeed depend ultimately on the truth of essential Christianity.

Henri Berr asserts that "historical research, every historical work rests on this postulate, more or less unconscious: that the course of human affairs is not vain. On this postulate is based, consciously but rashly, the work of philosophies of history. We must retain something of this, as hypothesis".[1] It is significant that a French historian, still clinging with mistaken caution to the Positivist idea of science without metaphysic, should realise that the historian, consciously or unconsciously, must affirm some meaning in history. The story of the past cannot be merely "a tale told by an idiot, full of sound and fury, signifying nothing". But we cannot help asking whether this postulate, this faith apart from which the very nerve of historical research would be cut, can be retained without affirming just that intimate connection of the eternal with the temporal which is of the essence of Christianity.

The term 'history' in our ordinary usage implies a process of significant change. In the first reference, the word should embrace the whole of the past experience of mankind, but it has at once to be narrowed down to the remembered past, or even to those features of the past which might be

[1] *La Synthèse*, p. 141.

described as memorable. For there is a distinction to be drawn between memories that are trivial and interesting though trivial, and memories that are momentous. The true centre of the historian's interest turns on events which, as we say, make history. If we analyse that phrase, we shall realise the nature of history as the subject-matter of a distinct science and shall also understand the demands made upon history as a science. Two comments on President Hoover's debt-moratorium may elucidate the theme. "The universal interest aroused by President Hoover's moratorium proves that an event of historic importance has occurred." The writer in the *Living Age* who offered this comment did not define historic importance more exactly, but a sentence from a leader in the *Manchester Guardian* gives the true interpretation. "One thing is certain: *things can never again be the same* as before the offer was made, and for that alone the President of the United States deserves the thanks of mankind." "Things can never again be the same"—there lies the essence of historic importance. Events that make history are happenings or actions which change the human situation. The same suggestion is conveyed by the old saying, "Happy is the country that has no history". It is a dubious beatitude. A people whose whole experience is exhausted in a placid routine is not truly blessed. "Because they have no changes, therefore they fear not God." But the implication of the term 'history' is not in doubt. It consists of events productive of significant change. Two characteristics of events of historic importance may be deduced from these examples. First, this having happened, things can never be the same again. We cannot revert to the *status quo ante*. Second, this having happened, it never can happen again. No exact repetition is desirable or even possible.

Readers of Lewis Carroll's romance, *Sylvie and Bruno*, will remember that when Sylvie imprudently gave Bruno an elective in his lesson hour, he chose history, because whereas lessons on other subjects have to be repeated history repeats itself. But for the modern historian, the truth 'history never repeats itself' takes precedence of the truth 'history repeats itself'. Clearly, if we use 'history' in its widest sense to include the whole of human experience, we have to take account of elements of repetition, of constant or relatively constant factors which tend to produce the same or similar results in human behaviour. If history in the broad sense did not repeat itself, there would be no material for what may be termed the natural sciences of man, anthropology, ethnology, psychology, sociology, economics and the like. But if history merely repeated itself, there would be nothing left for the historian proper to do. He would have no distinct task apart from the sociologist or psychologist, and yet in fact no extension of such sciences can ever make the historian superfluous. He is concerned with those elements of individuality, uniqueness, once-for-all-ness, the irreversible and non-repeatable, which escape the net of scientific generalisation and make the central interest of the human story.

If we keep this in mind, it is possible to resolve the ancient quarrel between the present Regius Professor of History in this University and his immediate predecessor over the status of Clio. Is she a muse who is still entitled to take her seat on Mount Helicon with her sisters, or is she a scientific researcher to be housed in a laboratory or a library?

"History is a science, no less and no more." Thus the late Professor Bury nailed his colours to the mast, claiming for history the same standards of impartiality or disinterestedness, the same endeavour after accuracy of measurement, as are characteristic of physics, claiming also that the historian must seek to establish relations of cause and effect just as the physicist does. On the other hand, in *Clio, a Muse*, G. M. Trevelyan, who now reigns in Bury's stead, gave a negative answer to the following question, "Ought emotion to be excluded from history on the ground that history deals only with the science of cause and effect in human affairs?" This alleged science, he argued, does not exist. History, unlike physical science, has no practical utility and cannot issue in predictions of coming events. The facts of the past are of interest in themselves, and not as the material of an exact science. To enter into them, the historian needs imagination and sympathy. So far from being unemotional and impartial, he must be able to put himself imaginatively into other people's situations and other people's skins. For great work in the field of history, the art of narrative is essential. Dull history is bad history, false history, and only a man with gifts of artistic appreciation and literary expression can be a great historian. The writing of history is more art than science.

This apparent opposition might be minimised by pointing out that imagination is required in ordinary scientific inquiries as well as in history, and that dullness in the presentation of results is not a virtue even in physicists.[1] The writing of a mathematical textbook is also an art, even if no particular muse presides over this form of literary

[1] I need hardly add that Bury was no defender of historians who despise or neglect literary form, and he himself possessed a delightful style as a writer.

activity. History is not devoid of practical utility, because it does not lead to inventions like the wireless or assist us to butter parsnips. But the real crux turns on the question, is history a science of cause and effect in human affairs, parallel to the natural sciences, or is the analogy of physical science misleading? On this issue, I hold that Professor Trevelyan is nearer the truth than Bury was. History is indeed a science, as Bury claimed, but it is not like other sciences. It is a science *sui generis*. If the primary aims of natural science be to arrive at valid generalisations and to explain away that which is strange and unusual by reducing apparent mysteries to complicated forms of simpler, more familiar processes, it is the business of history to handle those elements of particularity which cannot thus be reduced to something simpler, and which are necessarily ignored in the process of scientific generalisation. History is a science, but it is at once less and more than physical science. It is less of a science because it is inevitably less exact than physics. It is more of a science because it deals with aspects of human experience which must for ever lie outside the type of explanation sought in the physical sciences.

The essential difference between history as a department of knowledge, and physics, is well stated by Mr Bertrand Russell, in an article which he contributed to the *Independent Review* in 1904. "There is a further point against this view of history as solely or chiefly a causal science. Where our main endeavour is to discover general laws, we regard these as intrinsically more valuable than any of the facts which they interconnect.... But in history the matter is far otherwise.... Historical facts, many of them, have an intrinsic value, a profound interest on their own account, which makes them worthy of study, quite apart from any possibility of linking them together by means of causal laws."

Henri Poincaré illustrates the difference between the outlook of the historian and that of the physicist in a comment on a sentence from Carlyle. "Carlyle has written somewhere something like this. 'The fact alone matters: John Lackland has passed this spot, that is something to wonder at, a reality for which I would surrender all the theories in the world.' This is the language of the historian. The physicist would rather say, 'John Lackland passed this spot: that is nothing to me, since he will never pass this way again'." Carlyle no doubt is mistaken in suggesting that the bare fact is all that concerns the historian. An event is not of historical importance merely because it has happened once and can never happen again. Its importance must lie either in its significance as a link in a chain of still more significant happenings or in its embodying uniquely some intrinsic values. But it still remains true that the passing of King John by a particular spot on a particular day and hour is of no interest to the physicist because it can never happen again. It may be of great significance to the historian because it did actually happen once and only once.

It is a mistake to press the distinction between history and physics to a division. The historian must also deal in general laws where they are available. As Adrian Coates puts it, "history deals with two classes or levels of knowledge, the level of personality, of concrete events and causes, and the level of scientific generalisations and abstract causes".[1] The positions essential to the proper understanding of history as a science are these. First, history must embrace *both* levels of knowledge. Its claim to be a science does not depend on its confining its attention to the level of scientific generalisations and abstract causes, or on its power to reduce concrete events and causes to such generalisations. Second, its distinct position as a science depends on its recognition and understanding of the first level of knowledge. It is interesting to observe how Bury was driven to assert precisely this claim for history, and to break with Positivism on this issue. "The scope of history

[1] *Philosophy*, October 1933.

is to determine the stages in the *unique* causal series from the most rudimentary to the present state of human civilisation.... In the Positive Philosophy history is part of sociology: the interest in it is to discover the sociological laws. In the view of which I have just spoken, history is permitted to be an end in itself: the reconstruction of the genetic process is an end in itself."[1] Simply out of loyalty to his scientific task, and in strict fidelity to the facts he has to interpret, the historian is obliged to refuse the subordinate position offered to him in the Positive Philosophy.

The history of historiography in the nineteenth century is largely taken up with attempts to develop history as a science on the analogy of the physical sciences. In the twentieth century, historians have come to realise that such attempts must necessarily fail. Beyond the realm of scientific generalisations, the realm of relatively stable factors in human nature and its environment, the realm of measurable repetition, lies the realm of personality, of concrete events and causes, of the particular, the non-repeatable, the non-predictable, and the historian cannot accomplish his work without taking account of this latter realm. His task is to trace the development of a unique story, not to discover illustrations of general laws.

[1] *Darwinism and History*, 1909.

It would be easy to illustrate the modern historian's conception of his task from almost any field of historical inquiry.[1] An appeal to a Cambridge authority may lend appropriate support to my argument. As I shall have occasion in a later lecture to differ from Mr Butterfield in his estimate of Lord Acton's moralism, I am the more delighted to emphasise my agreement with him as to the nature of history and as to the aim of the historian. In the following sentences he seems to me to characterise justly the outlook and objective of the modern student of history.

"The value of history lies in the richness of its recovery of the concrete life of the past.... There is not an essence of history that can be got by evaporating the human and the personal factors, the incidental or momentary or local things, and the circumstantial elements, as though at the bottom of the well there were something absolute, some truth independent of time and circumstance.... When he describes the past the historian has to recapture the richness of the moments, the humanity of the men, the setting of external circumstances, and the implications of events; and far from sweeping them away, he piles up the concrete, the particular, the personal; for he studies the changes of things which change and not the

[1] See Note A at the end of the chapter.

permanence of the mountains and the stars. To recover the personality of Martin Luther in a full rich concrete sense—including of course all that some people might consider to be the accidents and non-essentials—is not only the aim of the historian, but is an end in itself; and here the thing which is unhistorical is to imagine that we can get the essence apart from the accidents."[1]

Once this is admitted, it is tempting to subsume this realm of the individual and personal, of concrete events and causes, under the rubric of contingency and to treat history as a chapter of accidents. Some such view of historical causation is adopted by M. Seignobos in the epilogue to his deservedly popular *Political History of Europe*. The decisive events of the critical years 1830, 1848, 1870 seemed to him to turn on personal idiosyncrasies, at once incalculable and in themselves trivial. Carried to its extreme, this becomes the "Cleopatra's-nose" interpretation of history. If Cleopatra had been snub-nosed, her charm might never have troubled Caesar and bewitched Antony. History thus turns on accidents of physical heredity. But while the course of history is constantly modified and sometimes seemingly determined by such accidental and trifling causes, Gasset is right when he says the true perspective for the historian is the

[1] H. Butterfield, *The Whig Interpretation of History*, pp. 68–9.

standpoint from which he can no longer see Cleopatra's nose.

The series of significant changes which form the
stuff of history consists primarily of man's creative
decisions, whereby something new comes into existence. History is a spiritual adventure, the
record of spiritual achievements. History is made
where men invent new tools, discover new resources and new ways of utilising resources both
old and new, where men make advances in political
thought and institutions, in conduct and character,
in scientific theory and philosophical speculation,
in literature, art and religion. Since the importance
of tools as factors in shaping history is often regarded as supporting a materialist conception of
history, it may be well to insist that man is a tool-
making animal because he is a spiritual rational
being. Every invention is a spiritual achievement.
Mr Hook, in his book, *Towards the Understanding of
Karl Marx*, recognises that to put tools in the fore-
ground, to say, as Marx himself said, the history
of man is the history of his tools, means the surrender of materialism. "A technological interpretation of history which separated technique
from antecedent social need in search for a
measurable *first* cause of social change, would have
to surrender its materialistic starting-point just as
soon as the simplified logic of that procedure were

pressed against it. For no technical change is made without a leading *idea* in the mind of the technician or inventor. Even if it be true that no great invention has ever been the sole creation of one mind, nevertheless the machine is projected in thought before it is embodied in stone and steel. The cause then would be some bright idea or happy thought in the mind of one or more persons, and we would be back to a thoroughgoing idealistic philosophy of civilisation."[1] How the association of technical invention with antecedent social need rehabilitates the materialistic starting-point and changes the essentially idealistic or spiritual character of invention itself is a little difficult to grasp. In truth, there is no possibility of a rational interpretation of any event of historic importance, in terms of any form of materialism, whether mechanistic or dialectical.

That the influence of the physical environment is an important factor in history is not of course in dispute. The development of what is called human geography is sufficient evidence that modern historians neither can nor do neglect this aspect of civilisation. Nor is the significance of events in the natural order—the Black Death, for example, or the earthquake in Lisbon—denied or belittled. That social needs are largely determined by the

[1] *Op. cit.* p. 129.

relation of men to their natural physical environment, and by changes in that environment wrought in accordance with strict physical laws of cause and effect, is a proposition which no historian need or dare question. But the unique development of civilisation from rudimentary primitive stages of culture to the present day cannot be explained in terms of the pressure of the physical environment. Social needs are not purely physical, or biological. History is made by man's relation to a world of values, and not simply by his relation to a natural order. Or I would rather say, history is made by the succession of man's attempts to realise values in and through the natural order. As Robert Bridges put it in a broadcast address, it seems as if that which is immortal seeks to be clothed upon with mortality. Man is the agent of such incarnation. "Only where a being is found which takes hold upon the requirements of the Ought and commits itself thereto, does the ideal law begin to press into the realm of the natural."[1] This happens whenever man discovers a truth, or creates artistically in virtue of a new vision of beauty, or embodies in character and action some ideal goodness. The rôle of the individual is at once apparent. History is not made by eccentrics, nor is it the record of individual peculiarities. It is rather the

[1] N. Hartmann, *Ethics*, vol. iii, p. 21.

outcome of those creative acts of individuals which make values available for mankind. An illustration from T. E. Hulme may help my argument. Take, "for instance, the effect produced by Constable on the English and French Schools of landscape painting. Nobody before Constable saw things, or at any rate painted them, in that particular way. This makes it easier to see clearly what one means by an individual way of looking at things. It does not mean something which is peculiar to an individual, for in that case it would be valueless. It means that a certain individual artist was able to break through the conventional ways of looking at things which veil reality from us at a certain point, was able to pick out one element which is really in all of us, but which before he had disentangled it, we were unable to perceive".[1] There is something unique in the individual's insight and achievement, but its greatness lies in the influence it exerts on others as a revelation of reality, in the extent and character of such influence.

It must, I think, be admitted that there can be no exact calculus of historic greatness or importance, and no final judgments based on historic data. Yet the historian must value. He cannot regard all the events of the past as on one dead level. And his

[1] *Speculations*, p. 150.

actual valuations and his scale of valuation are not arbitrary and subjective, even though they are not final. Surely de Burgh is right when he says, "He [the historian] values at every stage, selecting his theme and the relevant data in the light of a standard of historical significance. *The significance is objective*: it lies in the events themselves, not merely in their interest for a given historian under the present conditions of his enquiry.... The campaigns of Alexander, the foundation of New Rome upon the Bosphorus, the French or Russian revolutions, possess objective significance as landmarks in the course of history. They are important in themselves and no amount of familiarity with them can breed contempt".[1] But history requires to be rewritten in each generation, because in the light of the experience of each generation the exact significance of past events is altered. Some events advance, others dwindle in importance. Of complex events like revolutions their greatness may remain unimpaired, but our judgment on the balance of good and evil in them may change in the growing light or the lengthening shadows of their consequences.

Moreover, we have to face the strange fact that while history is a continuous process, to be viewed

[1] W. G. de Burgh, "Greatness and Goodness", *Proceedings of the Aristotelian Society*, N.S. vol. xxxii, p. 5.

as Bury said *sub specie perennitatis*, yet past events,
or the memory and appreciation of past events,
may act directly on the present, and not through
the medium of the influence of such events on the
intervening periods of time. A passage from A.E.
Taylor's Gifford Lectures enforces this truth. "In
the world of intelligent human action, the remembered past seems to be able to mould the
future directly and immediately, striking, so to
say, out of its remote pastness, even though there
has been no continuous persistence of itself or its
effects through the interval." A. E. Taylor proceeds to point out that in a purely physical world
this would be impossible. Only "in the life of
men, as intelligent and moral persons and not at
any lower level, we have a living past". Once again,
history is inexplicable in terms of materialism
or the physical sciences. But the point I would
stress is the difficulty of being sure that the significance of any past event is exhausted, and still
more the difficulty of restricting the influence of
past events to the line of their continuous persistence. An historian may make history, by
recovering forgotten facts. So, it was thought,
The Village Labourer, by J. L. and Barbara Ham-
mond, might make history. So Palacky's *History
of Bohemia* has shaped events today. So Karl
Marx's *Capital* makes history, not so much by its

philosophy as by its recovery of neglected historical material.

It will also be clear from this power of the remembered past to affect us in the present directly, that no stressing of the importance of historic continuity in Catholic Christianity (and I should not myself wish to question the real value of historic continuity) can ever confine the influence of the creative events enshrined in the records of the New Testament to the channel or channels in which we can trace the continuous persistence of such influence. No power on earth can prevent St Paul speaking directly to kindred spirits through the generations, however embarrassing the response of Marcion, or Augustine, or Luther, or John Wesley, or Karl Barth may seem to us to be. Such influence of the remembered past is indeed vital for the development of Christianity and Western civilisation.

If then we accept this view of history as a unique series of events, a genetic process which cannot be repeated and of which the decisive moments are creative acts of individuals embodying values with a wide or universal appeal, and if with such conceptions of the nature of history in our minds we turn to the problem of Christianity, we shall expect to find certain features of Christianity to be deserving of our closest attention, and it may be of our loyal adhesion.

We shall see at once that it is not necessarily absurd to insist on the importance of events in Palestine and to decline to identify the essence of Christianity with certain ideas, as expressed in a generalised philosophical form. Is it after all so strange that the attraction and interest of Christianity lie not so much in the ideas which it shares with other faiths and philosophies, but precisely in the embodiment of these ideas in concrete events in Palestine?

It is conceded that the popular appeal of Christianity is thus bound up with historicity. Walter Lippmann's endorsement of Dr Machen's criticism of Modernism[1] is thoroughly justified on this issue. "'Modernism', he [Dr Machen] says, 'is altogether in the imperative mood', while the traditional religion 'begins with a triumphant indicative.' I do not see how one can deny the force of this generalisation. 'From the beginning Christianity was certainly a way of life. *But how was the life to be produced?* Not by appealing to the human will, but by telling a story; not by exhortation, but by the narration of an event.' Dr Machen insists, rightly I think, that the historic influence of Christianity on the mass of men has depended upon

---

[1] The form of Modernism in question is that prevalent in the United States of America. The validity of the statement as a criticism of Modernism is not the point I want to emphasise.

their belief that an historic drama was enacted in Palestine nineteen hundred years ago during the reign of the Emperor Tiberius. The veracity of that story was fundamental to the Christian Church. For while all the ideal values may remain if you impugn the historic record set forth in the gospels, these ideal values are not certified to the common man as inherent in the very nature of things. Once they are deprived of their root in historic fact, their poetry, their symbolism, their ethical significance depend for their sanction upon the temperament and experience of the individual believer. There is gone that deep, compulsive, organic faith in an external fact which is the essence of religion for all but that very small minority who can live within themselves in mystical communion or by the power of their understanding."[1] The real force of the misnamed and misunderstood 'materialist' conception of history is expressed in this contention that a deep compulsive organic faith must rest on an external fact. Idealism in the air, ideas defined with academic precision, and held with academic detachment, do not make history, do not move men. Ideas must be actualised in events, embodied in persons, materialised in institutions, before they effectively shape human lives.

[1] *Preface to Morals*, p. 32.

This process of materialisation, or actualisation, must be necessary not only to appeal to the judgment of ordinary folk, but also to clarify the ideas themselves. It was said of the Hegelian dialectic movement that since the process of thought was logical in itself, it was hardly necessary for the events to go through the form of taking place. That is one reason for rejecting Hegelian dialectic as an adequate interpretation of history. The historical process must add something to the logical process. It cannot simply be the logical process repeated, for it then becomes superfluous. The indifference of the academic philosopher or the mystic to history means that something has been revealed to the babes which is hidden from the wise and prudent.

The gospel is good news of God, good news not so much concerning God's eternal nature in the abstract, but concerning God's action in time through which His eternal nature is expressed and understood. The Christian gospel is not adequately summed up in the phrases, "God is love", or "where love is, God is". It culminates in the assertion that God so loved the world that He gave His only Son. The nature of God's love is to be read not in generalities or in parables, but in the life and death of Jesus. New Testament writers, with a sound instinct, stress the fact that He died,

once for all. This event has changed and continues
to change the human situation. Things can never
be the same again, now that Christ has died.
Theologians have often shrunk from accepting the
full sweep of Paul's argument in Romans v, where
he compares the effect of Christ's death with the
effect of Adam's sin and fall.[1] But the Apostle
meant what he said, and he was right. Just as all
mankind is involved in Adam's fall, so all mankind
is affected by the righteous act of Christ. Of
course, all men are not saved, automatically, by
the fact of Christ's death. But all of us live in a
different and a better, though not necessarily an
easier world, because Christ has died. Whether we
like it or not, whether we recognise it or not, we
are all in debt to Him.

It is not likely that any of my readers accept any
of the once popular substitutionary doctrines of
the Atonement. The first series of Hulsean Lectures
in which as an undergraduate I took any interest
was devoted to this subject, and I shall always
be grateful to Archdeacon J. M. Wilson for offering
to my generation an interpretation of the death
of Christ, free from the moral objection attaching
to some earlier doctrines. Yet the old saints who

---

[1] "Just as one man's disobedience made all the rest sinners, so
one man's obedience will make all the rest righteous", Rom.
v. 19 (Moffatt's translation).

put their faith in what they called the finished work of Jesus were by no means mistaken. From the strictly historical standpoint, Jesus has done something for us which we could not do for ourselves and which presumably none but He could do. I may attempt a closer definition of this something in a later lecture. But in some degree the influence of Christ's death is suggested by a remark of the present Master of Balliol regarding the death of Socrates. "The death of Socrates stopped the moral rot of Greece." If that claim should seem exaggerated, at least it is clear that Socrates by dying convinced many young men that truth and justice were worth dying for. Under the influence of the martyrdom of Socrates, Plato would seem to have decided to give up political ambition in favour of education and philosophy. So with the death of Christ Himself. The Cross persuades men that love and humanity are worth dying for. Thus Paul was transformed from a fanatical persecutor into a true apostle of love. And to-day when there are so many ominous signs of moral retrogression, the Cross stands as the greatest single bulwark against a return to barbarism.

In any case, if we may trust the general drift of our argument, if history be the record of a unique series of critical or decisive changes, then the position which Jesus holds in history must be unique and significant. The primitive confessions of faith in Him, "Jesus is the Christ", "Jesus is Lord", were after all simple recognitions of His uniqueness and first attempts to define His significance. Modern interpretations of Jesus as leader or teacher or social reformer, as Rabbi or even as prophet, are in danger of trying to find His true significance in that which He has in common with others and which seems to be susceptible of imitation or repetition. That which is unique in Him is then dismissed as belonging to His age and as not permanently significant. But such an estimate inevitably does less than justice to the Jesus of history, and if I may say so, misses the whole point of the New Testament. To be the Christ, is to fill a position which only one can hold. As a mere matter of history, by any standard of objective significance, a greater than Solomon, a greater than Socrates is here.

NOTE A

THE MODERN VIEW OF HISTORICAL SCIENCE

A further example from a particular field will serve to illustrate the change of emphasis which has taken place in the realm of historical writing. M. Bréhier in the introduction to his history of philosophy (p. 29) thus contrasts the standpoint of the modern historian with that of Comte and Hegel:

"Comte et Hegel, et même Renouvier s'occupent de la philosophie et non des philosophes. Qu'ils considèrent ces représentations de l'univers qu'ils étudient, comme des cadres éternels imposés par la nature même de la raison, ou comme des sortes de représentations collectives, évoluant elles-mêmes collectivement et se transformant avec la société, ils font de la philosophie quelque chose d'impersonnel,[1] ou, du moins, l'expression personnelle que donne un philosophe des pensées de son temps n'est que l'accident; l'essentiel est ailleurs, dans ce *dictamen* rationnel ou social, sorte de déité, à laquelle se soumettent naturellement les consciences individuelles—fussent elles d'un Platon ou d'un Descartes.

Or l'histoire de la philosophie a évolué comme l'histoire en général; la minutie apportée à la recherche des sources ne s'expliquerait pas sans la volonté de l'historien d'arriver à ce qu'il y a d'individuel, d'irréductible, de personnel dans le passé; ses recherches seraient tout à fait inutiles, s'il s'agissait, comme autrefois, de déterminer des types ou des lois; à quoi bon un exemplaire nouveau d'un type déjà connu, si l'exemplaire n'avait son prix en lui-même et dans ce qui le distingue?

Ce goût de l'individuel, qui est peut-être encore le trait dominant de notre critique littéraire, nous fait voir le passé sous une perspective tout à fait nouvelle; ce ne sont plus ni des 'sectes' comme à la Renaissance, ni des 'systèmes' comme chez Cousin, ni des 'mentalités collectives' que vise à atteindre l'historien; ce sont des individus, dans toute la richesse nuancée de leur esprit; Platon, Descartes ou Pascal ne sont ni des

---

[1] En ce qui concerne Renouvier, certes le choix d'une des deux doctrines opposées est personnel et libre; mais les doctrines entre lesquelles le choix s'exerce sont tout à fait déterminées.

expressions de leur milieu ni des moments historiques, mais de véritables créateurs."

The italics in this quotation are mine. They emphasise the distinctive character of the modern historian's outlook. Professor J. S. Black's admirable critique of the leading eighteenth-century historians in his book, *The Art of History*, enforces the same truth. Essentially the same view of history is set forth in the essay contributed by Mr R. E. Balfour to Cambridge University Studies, and by Mr R. G. Collingwood in a pamphlet on the Philosophy of History, published by the Historical Association.

The bearings of the modern view of history on our Christian faith are thoughtfully surveyed by Mr W. J. Pennell in a book entitled *History and Modern Religious Thought*, a book which has not, in my judgment, received the attention it deserves.

Lecture II

GREAT MEN AND SOCIAL FORCES
IN HISTORY

And he goeth up into a mountain, and calleth unto him whom he
would: and they came to him.   MARK III. 13

Ye have not chosen me, but I have chosen you.   JOHN XV. 16

I AM conscious that in my first lecture I may
have suggested too definitely that the modern
historian's preoccupation with that which is
unique and individual is tantamount to a reasser-
tion of the predominant *rôle* of great men in
history. It would, however, be a misrepresenta-
tion of modern historical work to identify the
individual with the personal. The individual factors
which make history or which may be the subjects
of history are often in structure social. Social
groups of all kinds may be the most powerful influences in producing significant change, and they
certainly are essential in the realisation of such
changes, if not normally responsible for their initia-
tion. There is nothing to prevent a modern historian emphasising the part played by the crowd,
or by classes, or by other social units in determining the course of events. If history is not to

become the handmaid of the sociologist, at least the sociologist's contribution to the understanding of history has grown in importance.

There has been a necessary and healthy reaction against the conception of history as consisting of the biographies of great men. "Carlyle's *Heroes and Hero-Worship*", says Dr Schweitzer, "is not a profound book." Carlyle tends to isolate his heroes. They appear like so many bolts from the blue, or like a series of Melchizedeks, without father or mother. We are more conscious than we used to be of the intimate connection that so often subsists between a great man and the aspirations, the longings and the efforts of nameless multitudes. Theodore Merz has a fine passage at the beginning of his *History of European Thought in the Nineteenth Century*, where he speaks of the hidden life which lies behind the achievements the historian has to chronicle. "The vague yearnings of thousands who never succeed either in satisfying or expressing them, the hundreds of failures which never become known, the numberless desires which live only in the hearts of men or are painted only in their living features, the uncounted strivings after solutions of practical problems dictated by ambition or by want, the many hours spent by labourers of science in unsuccessful attempts to solve the riddles of nature—all these hidden and forgotten efforts form indeed the bulk of a nation's thought, of which only a small fraction comes to the surface, or shows itself in the literature, science, poetry, art, and practical achievements of the age. Equally important, though not equally prominent, this large body of forgotten thought has nevertheless been that which made the measure full, which heaped the fuel ready for the match to kindle; it constitutes the great propelling force which, stored up, awaits the time and aid of individual talent or genius to set it free."[1]

Troeltsch also reminds us that "there emerge in the prophet, in political genius, in artistic style, in the great historian's insight, in the system of the true philosopher, interpretations of the age and the future in which we need not always think of supermen in the sense of hero-worship, but can perceive the feeling, groping, longing and criticising of the masses directed to the same end". "This last", he adds, "is a condition precedent to the emergence of all heroes."[2] The achievements of great men

[1] Merz, *op. cit.* vol. I, p. 8.

[2] *Historismus*, p. 168: "Derart erwachsen im Propheten, im politischen Genie, im künstlerischen Stil, in der Intuition des grossen Historikers, in der Systematik des echten Philosophen, die Deutungen der Zeit und der Zukunft, wobei man nicht immer gleich an ungeheure Menschen im Sinne des Heroenkultus zu denken braucht, sondern auch das Sinnen, Grübeln, Sehnen und Kritisieren der Massen in diesem Sinne verstehen kann. Ja, dieses letztere ist ganz unzweifelhaft schon die Vorbedingung aller Heroen".

then are bound up with social influences, depend on opportunities which society provides and on the response which society or some elements in society make to the great man's lead.

Primitive Christianity itself is clearly a social phenomenon. Though I could not give to it the full meaning which he intends it to carry, I could accept the sentence of the Marxist, Karl Kautsky, "a world religion is not the product of an individual superman, but a social product".[1] The coming of Jesus is certainly not unrelated to the yearnings of the Jewish people, or to the less clearly defined aspirations of the Gentile world. The desire of all nations has gone to the making of Christianity. Again, as Dr Rendel Harris once said in lecturing on Martyrs and Apologists, "Jesus might have died in vain if He had not persuaded other men to die with Him and to die for Him". The achievement of Jesus is bound up with the faith of the Christian community, and the contribution of the community is felt to deserve increasing recognition to-day.

The new form of inquiry into gospel origins, known as Formgeschichte, is a significant tribute to the creative power of the early church. K. L. Schmidt rightly discerns in the vogue of Formgeschichte the influence of sociological interests.

[1] *Foundations of Christianity*, p. 42.

Why, he asks, did this new method seem to be in the air? "The so-called Formgeschichtliche way of regarding documents does not, like literary criticism, inquire for the *personalities* who have compiled this or that original document, but speaks of the *community*, from within whose entire life early Christian literature and particularly the gospels have taken shape. The earlier, more individualist way of regarding sources is being replaced by a more sociological. The scientific student too is an exponent of his age: this is his fate and his fortune. A new attitude in the philosophy of history is discernible by one who watches how the generations succeed to one another in scientific activities. It is intelligible that such a statement which resembles a confession should be combated or at least used to pillory a new method as dangerous or as insufficient. All the more clearly then must we affirm that the advance in methods of investigation here coincides with definite results of work in the field of the history of religion. In the history of religions, and consequently of religious literatures, the mass, the community has a greater importance than has previously been recognised."[1] Behind

[1] K. L. Schmidt, "Die Stellung der Evangelien in der allgemeinen Literaturgeschichte", in *Euchasterion*, p. 89: "Die sogenannte formgeschichtliche Betrachtungsweise fragt nicht so sehr wie die Literarkritik nach Persönlichkeiten, die diese oder jene Quellenschrift verfasst haben, sondern redet von der Gemeinde, aus deren

Mark's gospel stands not the personality of Peter but the primitive Christian community. Here we see not so much what Jesus was as a distinct figure in history, but what He was to His first devoted followers. We can no longer separate out the historic Jesus from the tradition in which the faith of the early church has enshrined Him.[1]

As I shall argue later, this new school of critical study does not justify a denial of the historicity of Jesus or of His creative influence. But the sociological fashion reflected in the rise of Formgeschichte lends colour to Christ-myth theories and indeed to all theories which regard Jesus as an historical but insignificant figure. The question raised by such theories and answered in the affirmative is this, May not the community be the real hero of the story?

Gesamtleben heraus die urchristliche und vor allen die Evangelien-Literatur geformt ist. Die frühere mehr individualistische Betrachtung wird von einer mehr soziologischen abgelöst. Auch der Wissenschaftler ist ein Exponent seiner Zeit; das ist Schicksal und Glück. Eine neue geschichtsphilosophische Einstellung ist spürbar für den, der beobachtet, wie sich auch im Wissenschaftsleben Generationen ablösen. Es ist begreiflich, dass ein solcher Satz, der wie ein Bekenntnis aussieht, bekämpft oder gar dazu benutzt wird, eine neue Methode als gefährlich oder als nicht belangreich hinzustellen. Um so deutlicher muss aber dann gesagt werden, dass der Gang der Forschung hier mit bestimmten Ergebnissen der religionsgeschichtlichen Arbeit zusammentrifft: in der Geschichte der Religionen und damit der religiösen Literaturen hat die Masse, die Gemeinde eine grössere Bedeutung, als das früher erkannt worden ist".

[1] Cf. Wellhausen, *Einleitung*, pp. 114, 115.

As a particular example of such theories I propose to examine Karl Kautsky's book, *Foundations of Christianity*. I choose it partly because, as Professor Norman Baynes observes in his select bibliography on *The Early Church and Social Life*, "there does not seem to be any considered criticism of these views in English", meaning by "these views" primarily the theories of Kautsky and Kalthoff. And the theories of the veteran leader of the German Social Democrats deserve consideration. Both the strength and the weakness of the Marxist interpretation of history are well represented in his study of the origins of Christianity, and since there is a revival of interest in this particular type of sociological approach, an examination of his positions should be well-timed.

Kautsky is persuaded that the clue to history is to be found in general laws of human behaviour, laws which govern men's conduct in regard to wealth in the first instance, and then in psychological and sociological laws which are closely related to this economic basis. To understand the past, we must learn "to isolate the essential and typical elements in the most varied historical phenomena from the non-essential and accidental elements, and to discover the true motives of men that lie behind their supposed motives".[1]

[1] *Op. cit.* p. 311.

The typical elements which are essential must be ideas entertained and activities pursued by masses of men, and indeed by successive generations of men. Flights of individual fancy or vision are insignificant accidents compared with these underlying constant social forces. "Individual persons may influence society and the delineation of prominent individuals is indispensable for a complete picture of their times. But when measured by historical epochs their influence is temporary at best, furnishes only the surface adornments which, while they may be the first portion of the structure that strikes the eye, reveal nothing to us concerning its foundation-walls."[1]

The resultant estimate of Jesus may be easily imagined. That such a person existed may readily be granted, because there are facts concerning his birth and death which his disciples were obviously anxious to gloss over and reinterpret. He clearly belonged to Galilee, because his birth can only be located at Bethlehem by a manifest artifice, and he must have been executed as an active rebel leader since the gospels are so concerned to declare his innocence and to exonerate the Roman authorities. But the teaching attributed to Jesus has no necessary or probable connection with him. The gospels, which have as much or as little historic value as

[1] *Op. cit.* p. 43.

the *Iliad* or the *Nibelungenlied*, give us no definite information about the life and doctrine of Christ, but much concerning the social character, the ideals and aspirations of the primitive Christian congregation. Actually in the gospel records "there is not a single Christian thought that requires the assumption of a sublime prophet and superman to explain its origin, not one thought that cannot be pointed out before the time of Jesus in 'pagan' or Jewish literature".[1] Moreover, the teachings are so diverse and inconsistent, that they must derive from divergent and competing groups, Judaistic and Hellenistic, within the primitive Christian community. Such groups twist the traditions concerning Jesus to their own side. Jesus is an empty vessel into which each theologian may pour his own intellectual equipment.[2]

If Kautsky dismisses Jesus as teacher, he likewise discounts him as magnetic personality. He will not hear of the argument which traces belief in the resurrection of Jesus to "the particularly profound impression made by his personality". "If it was only the personal impression made by Jesus that produced the faith in his resurrection and his divine mission, this faith would necessarily become weaker as personal recollection of him died away and the number of people who had been in per-

[1] P. 326.   [2] P. 38.

sonal contact with him decreased." "No one can leave behind a memory of his personality beyond the circle of those who have been in personal contact with him, unless he has produced a creation which is capable of making an impression quite apart from his person, be it an artistic creation, an edifice, a reproduction, a musical composition, a work of literature: or a scientific achievement, a methodically arranged collection of data, a theory, an invention, a discovery: or finally a political or social institution of some kind or other, produced by him or at least with his distinguished cooperation."[1] In the case of Jesus, either he was the founder of a communist organisation or he was connected with such an organisation in such a way that as the organisation grew, his importance as presumed founder grew along with it. "It was not the faith in the resurrection of the Crucified which created the Christian congregation and gave it its strength, but on the contrary it was the vigour and strength of the congregation that created the belief in the continued life of the Messiah."[2]

Starting from such principles, Kautsky must attribute the formation and spread of the organisation, not to the influence of a person, but to certain essential features of the social economic life of the time. He begins, rightly, with the wider world of

[1] P. 375.   [2] P. 378.

the Roman Empire. In his masterly analysis of the economic structure of the Empire, he reveals the strength of the Marxist approach to historical problems. The institution of slavery rendered the position of the peasant-farmer and the free artisan more and more difficult. There resulted the formation in Rome and other big cities of a *Lumpenproletariat*—a body of unemployed living on the charity of the State or the rich. Such a proletariat desired not work but bread and games. Its revolutionary aims did not envisage the abolition of slavery but only a redistribution of wealth among free citizens. Reliance on slave-labour both in agriculture and in handicrafts led to a decline in economic efficiency. Technique made no progress, and indeed rather deteriorated. Stagnation in the economic life of society is reflected in the general feeling of stalemate which pervaded ancient society when it lost its nerve. All the moral, intellectual, and religious tendencies of the first century A.D. are intimately connected with the fundamental structure of a slave-economy.

The development of the religious nationalism of the Jews is dependent throughout on economic factors. The Jews, unlike the Greeks and other peoples, were weak in the graphic and plastic arts. Hence in their polytheistic stage, their gods never became distinct figures, and their weakness in arts and crafts made the transition to monotheism easier for the Jews. It is characteristic of Kautsky, and indeed of Marxists generally, that the alternative possibility is not considered, the possibility, namely, that an incipient monotheism coupled with a prohibition of the use of graven images may have hindered the rise of graphic and plastic arts among the Jews. But Kautsky could not admit this, because monotheism is developed only in urban centres by philosophers. It depends on the growth of trade and city-life. National consciousness is also fostered by trade. The great advance in Jewish religious life and thought was due to the exile. In exile, the Jews came to depend more on trade and commerce, and trade develops those faculties of abstraction and generalisation which lie at the basis of scientific study and philosophic inquiry. In a great city like Babylon some philosophers must have elaborated monotheistic doctrines, and no doubt the priesthood treasured an esoteric monotheism. From Babylon the Jews must have derived a belief in one God, along with the myths of creation and the flood. "We may assume that the Jewish priesthood probably acquired from the highly developed Babylonian priesthood...a higher and more spiritual conception of divinity, *even though we have no direct evidence to this effect.*"[1] Subsequent to

[1] P. 231. Italics mine.

the exile, the Jews as a trading people tended to multiply, and since all merchants on the Marxist hypothesis are essentially an exploiting class, the more Jewish traders multiplied, the less popular they became with other nations. Their religious traditions took permanent shape in their sacred writings, edited and largely written after the exile. Their religious institutions centred at Jerusalem, and a vested interest in their religion naturally developed. "The Jews in Palestine regarded their God as the means by which they lived."[1] Their devotion to the national faith had a deep economic root. When the tribute demanded by the Seleucid monarchy became too heavy, the Jews rebelled, and "like every decaying system, this system [the empire of the Seleucids] increased its oppressive measures, which naturally produced resistance". The successful Maccabean revolt implanted hopes of independence which survived the downfall of the Maccabean state.

Brought within the frontiers of the Roman Empire, Palestine shared the conditions that prevailed throughout the Empire. Her workers felt the pressure of the competition of slave-labour, and the landless and workless form a menacing source of disturbance and revolution. "In the time of Christ there was not a single large city that did

[1] P. 272.

not possess a numerous *Lumpenproletariat*. But after Rome, Jerusalem probably contained the largest proletariat of this description, at least relatively: for in both cities this rabble was collected from the whole Empire."[1] The economic oppression from which the Jews suffered was due to far-reaching economic causes, but they attributed it largely to Roman rule. If they could throw off the yoke of Rome, all would be well. The internal class-conflict tended to be masked by or merged in the national opposition to Rome. The activists in Israel were the bandits of Galilee (recruited from petty peasants and shepherds who were being exploited) and the proletarians of Jerusalem. These elements united to form the Zealot party, and Christianity arose from these rebellious strata and was in its beginnings a violent revolutionary movement. Kautsky anticipates the essential contentions of Robert Eisler. The cleansing of the Temple-courts could only have come about after violent street-fighting. Either the episode is a myth, or it was a more serious military operation than appears from the gospel narrative. That Jesus appealed to the rebels is clear from the fact that he called sinners and not righteous men to his side. Luke certainly says he called them *to repentance*, but that is a manifest watering down of the truth. Jesus

[1] P. 297.

recruited his following from the revolutionaries, and he was put to death as a revolutionary leader. The reference to his coming to send not peace but a sword, and the advice to his disciples to buy swords, are further indications of the original character of the movement which were so firmly fixed in the tradition that no pacifist editing could get rid of them.

One wing of the proletarians developed this religious jingoism. Another wing sought to remedy economic distress by a communist organisation. Probably the Essenes owe their origin to this attitude. The Essenes may be presumed to spring from the proletarians, though tradition tells us nothing on the subject, because they practised communism—a proletarian remedy for proletarian ills—and because they believed in Fate, and determinism is the creed of oppressed classes who are not their own masters. Jesus would seem to have succeeded in uniting some elements of Essenian communism with the violent revolutionary enterprise of the Zealots.

What evidence is forthcoming in favour of this thesis? The New Testament shows that the primitive Christian congregation was characterised by savage class-hatred against the rich. The parable of Dives and Lazarus, the story of the rich fool, the woes on the rich, and above all the terrific denunciation of the wealthy in the epistle of James, show how the land lies. "Few are the occasions on which the class-hatred of the modern proletariat has assumed such fanatical forms as that of the Christian proletariat."[1]

This bitter hatred was softened down as soon as educated and wealthy persons joined the movement in any numbers. Matthew must be later than Luke. It moderates Luke's socialism, because the wealthy have begun to come in.

In the next place, the first Christian congregations practised communism. We have two glowing accounts in Acts of this essential feature of the movement. Jesus himself and his disciples are said to have lived on a common fund of which Judas was treasurer, and surrender of one's property was a condition of discipleship. But this communism was simply a sharing of consumable goods, indeed it was little more than the provision of common meals. Such a communism of consumption is all that the *Lumpenproletariat* understands or desires. The members of this class do not know how to organise production on a communistic basis. And it is a curious fact that the gospels say nothing in praise of work.[2] When Jesus does refer to labour,

---

[1] P. 329.
[2] P. 346; cf. p. 124: "The gospels have no place for work: in this they all agree, in spite of all their contradictions".

he does so in most disdainful terms. Life on the lily and sparrow basis as commended in the Sermon on the Mount is life without toil. This is proof positive that Christianity arose among the *Lumpenproletariat* whose visions of the future and whose social programmes contain no place for work.[1] Their expectations of the kingdom of heaven on earth are marked by emphasis on the pleasures of the table.

Communism is always antagonistic to the family, and we find primitive Christianity committed to the destruction of family ties. The attitude of Jesus towards his mother and brethren, and the promises made to those who surrender wife and children for the kingdom, attest this aspect of communism. It is legitimate to suspect that primitive Christian communism issued either in an ascetic discouragement of marriage or in irregular sexual connections. A curious statement in Campanella's *City of the Sun* adduces the authority of Saint Clement the Roman for the view that by the arrangement of the Apostles even their wives had to be owned in common. The cosmic mysteries in which according to the *Didache* a prophet might indulge without ecclesiastical censure may have

[1] I understand that in Russia young communists may grow up without hearing of the Good Samaritan; but they will know about Martha and Mary, because the incident shows how Jesus disparaged work.

involved some sexual irregularity, and when Paul claims to exercise the privilege of an apostle in leading about with him a sister, "it is impossible that a legally married wife should here be meant by the Apostle's defence of his 'freedom'".[1]

The crucifixion appears to have initiated a separation between Jewish nationalism and proletarian class-antagonism, which was completed by the events of the year 70. The common hatred of Rome and the rich is polarised into two distinct currents. The international or cosmopolitan appeal of the Christian movement lay in its emphasis on the class-struggle. It appealed to the *Lumpenproletariat* in every city, alike by its practical communism and by its hope of release from oppression through the coming kingdom of heaven.

By a dialectic movement, Christianity was gradually transformed into its opposite. From being the most magnificent apologia for communism, it became the meanest defence of property. After the *débâcle* of 70, when Jerusalem fell in blood and terror, it ceased to be violently revolutionary and became pacifist and submissive to the State. It lowered its demand for the surrender of private property and retained a dismal and limited form of charity. It ceased to be a democracy in which all participated on an equality, and became an

[1] P. 349 n.

institution governed by a clerical hierarchy with strong vested interests. It ceased to expect or demand a good time here, and became a morbid other-worldly religion, the customary opiate of the people.

So rapid a sketch cannot make this account of Christian origins probable, especially to those who are unfamiliar with this way of approach. As worked out in detail by Kautsky, it seems much more plausible, and it does emphasise social and economic factors of real importance, to which Christianity was inevitably related. Dr Klausner's admirable chapter on the economic conditions prevailing in Palestine in the time of Jesus bears out Kautsky's analysis in many important particulars. Yet if one remains unconvinced, one is not necessarily blinded by bourgeois prejudice.

All such constructions must pass the test of ordinary literary criticism. On what principles does the historian handle his sources? Is he consistent in his use of them? Does he interpret them correctly in detail? To press such questions is not an attempt to evade an unwelcome and novel theory by depreciating the author's scholarship. It was said of Lightfoot that in his *Essays on Supernatural Religion* he attacked and riddled the writer's learning but did not face his main contentions. Certainly Lightfoot deliberately and justifiably confined his attention to Mr Cassels' parts 2 and 3, in which the historical evidence was reviewed; but it could fairly be argued that the defects revealed in the historical work sufficed to discredit the rationalist presuppositions from which Mr Cassels set out. St Augustine tells us that his doubts about Manichæism began when he discovered the unscientific character of their scriptural exegesis.[1] No form of the Christ-myth theory can survive this test. As Dr Schweitzer observes, "It is no hard matter to assert that Jesus never lived. The attempt to prove it, however, infallibly works round to produce the opposite conclusion". This dialectic process whereby the Christ-myth theory discredits itself rests on the simple fact that you cannot attempt to prove the theory without mishandling the evidence.

Kautsky shares with the late J. M. Robertson and other champions of the Christ-myth hypothesis an unwillingness to acknowledge the priority of Mark's gospel. Yet if there is one conclusion more certain than any other in the field of Synoptic criticism, it is the discovery that in Mark we come nearer to the primitive form of the traditions concerning the life and ministry of Jesus than we do in Luke or Matthew. Mr J. M. Robertson used

[1] Cf. *Confessions*, bk. v, ch. 11. It is worth noting that the Manichæans treated difficult passages as interpolations by Judaisers. Any arbitrary and unscientific system of interpretation must defend itself by positing endless interpolations.

habitually to start from Matthew; Kautsky as habitually starts from Luke. In neither case is the starting-point justified, and in neither case is justification felt to be necessary. A scientific historian cannot take his responsibilities so lightly.

Luke is the oldest gospel, because it contains Dives and Lazarus. "The various writers who collaborated in producing Mark omitted all the unfavourable parts which they possibly could omit, such as the story of Dives and Lazarus, condemnation of the inheritance dispute (Luke xii. 13 ff.)."[1] Mark's gospel is here supposed to be an abbreviation of Luke, just as Augustine once regarded it more plausibly as an abbreviation of Matthew! Mark is later than Luke and is an adaptation of Luke's material to please the wealthy and the educated. Yet on indisputable literary evidence we know that Mark is earlier than Luke and that Mark is in style and character the popular proletarian gospel, while Luke is written for the educated and the well-to-do. We cannot but distrust a bias which leads Kautsky to ignore such obvious facts. Nor does he consistently hold to his own curious view of Mark. When it suits his purpose, as in the case of the saying, "I came not to call the righteous, but sinners", it is Luke who makes a conciliatory addition to an offensive saying,

[1] P. 330.

and the writers who collaborate in producing Mark have not in this instance omitted something they found in Luke. Kautsky regards as primitive whatever features of any gospel happen to fit in with his preconceived picture of Christian origins. This is not a scientific procedure.[1]

As I shall have occasion to note in the sequel examples of doubtful interpretations of particular passages, I may pass from Kautsky as literary critic and proceed to consider other features of his work as an historian. It is the merit of Marxism to have insisted on the importance of economic factors in history, but in this system the factors labelled economic are conceived either so rigidly as to be inadequate for the purpose of explaining events, or so loosely as to cease to be genuinely and strictly economic. Since every other side of man's life and thought must have some association with and some degree of dependence on the production and distribution of material wealth, it is very natural to assume that this economic factor, being necessary, is in some way final and determinative of the course of history. Any theory of economic determinism must indeed go beyond the magnificent simplicities of the original Marxist faith which can see nothing in history but class-conflicts and those conflicts waged ever between oppressors

[1] See Note B at the end of the chapter.

and oppressed.[1] Even Kautsky provides ample evidence of the inadequacy of the materialist conception of history as defined in the Communist Manifesto. For him, the *Lumpenproletariat* and the rich unite in oppressing the slave-class, and the modern proletariat will hardly remember with pride the work-shy ancient proletariat whose savagery, sensuality, selfishness and superstition Kautsky depicts so unsparingly. But throughout the book, the working of economic influence, though rightly emphasised, is misconstrued, and the priority of economic reasons for men's actions too readily assumed.[2]

This preoccupation with economic factors inevitably involves Kautsky in a misunderstanding of primitive Christianity. What is the true character of the communism described so glowingly in Acts? Incidentally, Kautsky, who realises that Luke exaggerates the harmony of the Apostolic church and sees things *couleur de rose*,[3] should have been on his guard against assuming that the communism described in Acts was as far-reaching and important as Luke suggests. All we are entitled to deduce as historic fact is that the charitable duties

[1] The Russian Marxists discard Kautsky and regard Christianity as a movement of the oppressed slave-class, not of the *Lumpenproletariat*. Kautsky's emphasis on the *Lumpenproletariat* is clearly not justified.
[2] See Note C at the end of the chapter.
[3] Cf. Kautsky, *op. cit.* p. 385.

which were regarded as obligatory by the whole
Jewish community and not devised by the proletariat to relieve their poverty were undertaken
by the primitive Christian community for their
own members, that this Christian charity took the
form of a common table which was the more attractive because it expressed a feeling of brotherhood and possessed a religious significance, and
that at the first in their enthusiasm and possibly
expecting the end of the age, wealthier converts
enriched the common fund by selling their property. There was no binding rule enforcing the
surrender of private possessions, and there was no
organisation of common households such as were
characteristic of the Essenes. It is doubtful whether
such an experiment should be called 'communism'
at all, and in any case it was not, so far as we
know, an experiment made by the *Lumpenproletariat,* and it was not advocated and imitated
throughout the cities of the Empire as a solution
of the problem of poverty, in the way in which
the experiment of the Rochdale pioneers spread
through Great Britain in the nineteenth century.
The spirit of brotherhood was diffused, but this
particular embodiment of it was not proclaimed
or adopted as essential.[1]

[1] On p. 345, Kautsky undertakes later on in his book to meet
the objection that this communist experiment is reported only

The other characteristics to which Kautsky appeals as evidence that primitive Christianity is a movement among the *Lumpenproletariat* are clearly misunderstood. The parable of Dives and Lazarus is cited as evidence of savage class-hatred, but Kautsky forgets that the terms 'rich' and 'poor' have in Judaism of the time of Jesus become so closely associated with 'sinful' and 'pious' that they are no longer purely economic terms. Matthew's 'poor in spirit' gives the true meaning of 'Blessed are ye *poor*' in Luke. The rich were judged offenders from the standpoint of national religion; they had constantly compromised with Hellenism and with the political power of Rome. The 'rich' were frequently condemned on religious grounds in Rabbinic teaching, and the Rabbis certainly were not the mouthpiece of the *Lumpenproletariat*. The motif of the Dives and Lazarus story is found in Egyptian and Jewish sources[1] and does not possess the significance which Socialists have constantly read into it. As it stands, the interest in the story is deflected from the rich-and-poor issue and concentrated on the question of the sufficiency of the revelation through Moses and

of Jerusalem. Unhappily he never fulfils his undertaking. All he offers his readers is an argument from analogy, a must-have-been, with which he attempts to make up for lack of evidence.

[1] See Dr J. M. Creed's commentary on Luke's Gospel, *in loc.*, and compare also V. Taylor, *The Formation of the Gospel Tradition*, p. 104 f.

the prophets. Though it is found in Luke's special source which is now esteemed an early and valuable authority, its claim to be part of the propaganda of the first Christian community is doubtful, and its claim to be the centre of that propaganda is non-existent.[1] The denunciations of the rich in the epistle of James are prompted in all probability by the experience of religious persecution, and do not reflect in particular the class-hatred of the proletariat. Kautsky makes much of the absence of any reference to work in the gospels, and he discovers in the teaching of Jesus a contempt for work which he attributes to the mentality of the city-beggars. They do not want work, and so Jesus is represented as depreciating it. Their communism is confined to consumption and contains no plan for production. This silence of the gospels is easily explained on other grounds. Jesus was not creating an economic organisation for society, and so he had no occasion to insist on the importance of work. Moreover, he belonged to a nation, the Jewish nation, and to a class within it, the artisan class, both of which took the duty of manual labour for granted. Jesus had no occasion to enforce a duty that was not neglected. Work-shy members of the *Lumpenproletariat* did join the primitive Christian church, and their idleness was at once rebuked. The

[1] Cf. Bultmann, *Jesus*, p. 97.

first letter to the Thessalonians may be the earliest document in the New Testament, and in it Paul insists that his converts shall work with their hands. This is no innovation. It is primitive Christianity.[1]

As there was no contempt for labour, so there was no destruction of the family in the primitive Christian movement. The passages which Kautsky cites about hating father and mother, wife and child, are not parallel to the regulation of the Essenes in renouncing marriage for a communist fellowship. Every missionary, every prophet and social reformer, everyone who has to leave an old faith and adopt a new, indeed every persecuted communist agitator to-day, knows well enough what Jesus meant, and knows well enough that these sayings have no connection with any renunciation of the family and family obligations required by the exigencies of communist society. For the rest, Kautsky's evidence is either worthless or irrelevant or misinterpreted. The same letter to Thessalonica which disproves one proletarian communist characteristic suffices to disprove the other.[2]

---

[1] Cf. I Thessalonians iv. 11, 12: "Also, endeavour to live quietly, attend to your own business, and—as we charged you—work with your hands, so that your life may be correct in the eyes of the outside world and self-supporting" (Moffatt's rendering).

[2] I Thessalonians iv. 3 f.: "It is God's will...that each of you should learn to take a wife chastely and honourably..." (Moffatt's rendering).

The theory that Jesus was a rebel leader and executed as such, after an ill-conceived *coup de main*, has at least this in its favour, that Jesus can hardly have avoided contact with the rebellious strata. On one occasion the Galilean crowd would have taken him by force and made him king, and his arrest must have been motived either by some actual *émeute* or by the fear of it in the minds of the religious and political leaders. Yet it is hard to justify the assumption that the first followers of Jesus were violent revolutionaries and only finally abandoned violence when it was proved futile after the *débâcle* of 70.[1] The case for revolutionary violence as characteristic of Christianity in its beginnings is, after all, very flimsy, even more flimsy than Weingarten's case for attributing military sympathies and activities to the Quakers under the Commonwealth. That Jesus came to call sinners is no appeal to revolutionary violence. A rebel leader would never have said, "I have come not to bring peace, but a sword". In his case, *cela va sans dire*. A leader who was essentially a peacemaker and who knew the danger of sentimentality might express himself in such a manner. Whatever else the passage about the two swords may mean,

---

[1] Incidentally, Kautsky has forgotten that Jewish rebel activities continued till the time of Barcochba and Hadrian. Why should the followers of Jesus have become pacifist about A.D. 70 and not either before or much later?

no rebel leader in his senses would have regarded them as sufficient for a military *coup d'état*. The direction to the disciples to buy swords may mean that each man must look to his own defence. It may be an endorsement of the practice of the Essenes, who, though opposed to war and all preparations for war, yet carried defensive weapons when travelling.[1] Probably the advice to the disciples is very much on a par with the well-known answer of George Fox to William Penn on the question of wearing his sword, "Wear it as long as thou canst". This obscure incident affords no basis for refusing to recognise the peaceful character of primitive Christianity. The choice of Barabbas in place of Jesus is inexplicable if Jesus were a rebel leader of the same violent type as Barabbas. If men hoped that Jesus would head a violent revolution and he refused, the revulsion of feeling in the Jewish mob and the final rejection of Jesus become intelligible.

Kautsky in his introduction rightly claims that in historical studies the mere observer is at a disadvantage compared with the man who has taken some active part in the kind of movement whose history he is studying. In the same way, Lord Acton thought the writer of political history needed the qualification of diplomatic or parliamentary

[1] See Ginsburg, *The Essenes*, p. 42, n. 27.

experience. Renan once said, "If you would form an idea of the first Christian congregations, drop in at the local section of the International Workers' Association".[1] Kautsky himself is qualified by his life-long devoted service to the German Social Democratic movement. But there are limitations to his experience. He would understand primitive Christianity better, if he had been in South Wales during the 'Evan Roberts' revival, or if he had ever worked with a Primitive Methodist church, or attended a negro camp-meeting, or stood at a street corner with a Salvation Army band. He has participated in popular movements with a social-economic purpose, and he assumes that Christianity must have been essentially a popular movement of this character. This insistence on the priority of the economic issue misleads him, so that with some acuteness he fastens on features in the record which are secondary and treats them as fundamental, and reads into the record features that are not there.

Somewhat in the same way Kautsky misses the essential in history precisely because he confines himself to the general and the typical. He may be right in thinking that philosophic reflection arises in cities, when the development of trade permits the formation of a leisured class, and that

[1] Cited in *Foundations of Christianity*, p. 463.

such reflection leads men to realise or affirm the
unity of nature, the unity of the self, and the unity
of God. Yet as he himself sees, the advance of
trade and the growth of urban centres at best
develop the necessary ability for disinterested scientific inquiry, but do not ensure its application. To
analyse the economic conditions which make
scientific inquiry and philosophical reflection possible, and to show that these conditions were
realised in Miletus and Ephesus in the sixth century B.C., affords no explanation of that unique
movement in history which we know as Greek
Thought. Philosophic monotheism does not necessarily and inevitably develop in every city-centre
which has a leisured class, much less a priesthood.
Kautsky's thesis as to the origin of Jewish monotheism is adopted without evidence, confessedly,
and in deference to a dubious generalisation.
Actually Jewish monotheism owes much to Amos,
a countryman who did not derive his ideas of God
from Babylon or any other city-centre. And the
monotheism of Israel has a unique quality because
it is developed through the unique experiences of
particular persons, and not through trade and
cities. But Kautsky cannot admit this. He must
be able to reduce the religion of Israel to type.
Therefore he cannot understand it.

And so with Christianity itself. "We have seen

w   5

that several ingredients of Christianity, monotheism, messianism, belief in the resurrection, the
Essenian communism, arose among the Jews, and
that a part of the lower classes of this people found
the most satisfactory expression of its desires and
aspirations in a combination of these elements."[1]
This is both true and false. Stated in these general
terms, it is false. Christianity was not a combination of these elements. It was a belief not in
monotheism but in a new act or word of the one
living God. It was a belief not in messianism but
in an actual messiah. It was a belief not in the
Pharisaic doctrine of resurrection but in a risen
person. It was not an adaptation of Essenian
communism but a brotherhood united in a common faith and hope and practising a large-hearted
charity towards one another. Such a combination
of elements is no philosophical construction, is no
party programme, is no composite amalgam of
popular desires and aspirations.[2] It could only
come into being through the emergence of a personality, and moreover of a personality who did
not express the ordinary desires and aspirations of

[1] *Op. cit.* p. 408.
[2] Cf. Johannes Müller, *Jesus as I see Him*, p. 13: "The longing
of the people after the Kingdom may have reached its purest
and deepest, but that longing could not of itself engender the
birth of a new creature. Longing is the capacity to receive, but
it takes more than receptivity to create".

the common people but to whom they looked up as other and higher than themselves.

Kautsky's attempt to lay bare the foundations of Christianity while refusing to recognise Jesus as the cornerstone, illustrates the truth of Croce's sentence, "Let him who cuts individuals out of history but pay close attention, and he will perceive that either he has not cut them out at all, as he imagined, or he has cut out with them, history itself". The typical elements which the sociologist discovers in history and embodies in empirical rules, wrongly regarded as natural laws, are not indeed unimportant, but they can never be equated with the essential element in history. I am sure Troeltsch is right when he says that the economic political background is important for cultural contents, but culture is not simply the reflection of such background, and also when he adds, "the fascination of sociology for the dilettanti will have ceased as soon as the superstition is surrendered that we can with its help explain the rise of higher spiritual interests and values". Kautsky, like other sociologists, Marxist and non-Marxist, persistently mistakes a description of the background for a discovery of the foundations.

Sociological theories of the origins of Christianity are necessarily incomplete and unsatisfying. Jesus himself cannot be explained as the expression either of the social aspirations of economically oppressed classes or of the more distinctly religious longings of mankind under the Roman Empire. The elements of truth in such theories find their account, as I have already suggested, in the modern type of criticism which emphasises the influence of the church on the formation of the gospel traditions. It would be impossible at the close of a lecture to outline the methods and findings of the new school of criticism. For English readers, an admirable survey, at once sympathetic and judicious, may be found in Vincent Taylor's book, *The Formation of the Gospel Tradition*.[1] It is too early yet to speak confidently of its results, but so far as this form of analysis has gone, it suggests that the Synoptic gospels are built up on stories as remembered by humble believers, that they show the characteristics and limitations of literature destined for the common people rather than for the educated. The closest analogies in general literature might be found not in the *Iliad* and the *Nibelungenlied*[2] but in the records of early monasticism in Egypt, in mediæval legends of the saints,

[1] Dr Easton's earlier book, *The Gospel before the Gospels*, should not be overlooked.

[2] Even as a Marxist, Kautsky should have seen that the social-economic background of the gospels is quite different from the environment to which the epics of Greeks and Germans are related.

and particularly in the traditions regarding St Francis. That the gospels are not strictly parallel to Xenophon's reminiscences of Socrates and do not conform to classical biographical models certainly does not discredit them. They may be more ingenuous and trustworthy because they are not conscious portraits and do not set out to be 'lives' of Jesus. In the formation of the traditions there is no trace of wholesale fabrication and wilful distortion and transformation of the details, but the tradition may be constantly affected by limitations of the community's interests, by the desire to relate details to situations in the life of the church rather than in the life of Christ, by lapse of memory, or by misunderstanding. But when we take these factors into consideration, we discover the remarkable fact that the Synoptic traditions have been affected only to a slight degree by the subsequent interests of the early church. Much less is read back into the gospels than we might expect, and much is retained in the gospels which finds little or no echo in later church teaching and discussion. The use of the title 'Son of Man' is a case in point. The title is seldom in evidence outside the gospels. It has been suggested that some obscure group employed the phrase 'Son of Man' as a designation of Jesus, but the suggestion is intrinsically difficult. If it be true, we must suppose a phase or a faction in Jewish Christianity (for the title cannot be Hellenistic in origin) so powerful as to thrust its favourite title for Jesus into a dominating position in the gospel tradition, and so short-lived as to disappear completely from later church history. To recognise the title as coming from Jesus Himself, as His self-designation, or perhaps as His reaffirmation of Daniel's conception of the community of the saints of God, is to put oneself in line with fact. Precisely because the gospels are proletarian documents, precisely because the community is in some sense the author, the process of formation of the tradition is quite different from that supposed by Kautsky. So far from theologians attributing to Jesus any teaching they please, we see groups of simple people treasuring their memories of His words and deeds, and if they uncritically attribute to Jesus utterances of Christian prophets or sayings and stories from other sources, their selection is still governed by a definite impression of what is in character and they retain intact His leading thoughts and phrases when their own faith in Him was being expressed in other terms. Even when he wrote in 1908, Kautsky's appeal to pagan and Jewish parallels was irrelevant and antiquated. Parallels may be cited to every recorded teaching of Jesus, but the originality of that teaching and the impression of one man's mind behind it all are not thereby in the least affected. Dr Montefiore knows much better than Kautsky how rich and extensive are the Jewish parallels to the teaching of Jesus, but he never questions the originality of Jesus. The criterion of *Unerfindlichkeit*, uninventableness, is indeed sub-jective and difficult to apply, and yet, as Vincent Taylor says, it is indispensable. The parable of the prodigal son is the work of a sublime prophet, and cannot be otherwise accounted for. It is certainly not the wisdom of common sense. A Chinese hearing the story for the first time merely remarked of the father in the parable, 'More fool he!' A well-known story of a returning prodigal in Buddhist sources depicts a father acting with proper caution under the circumstances.[1] The father hides from the son and puts him to a series of tests, until the genuineness of his conversion permits his full restoration. To many this form of the story will seem much more rational and sensible, as indeed it is. But then in Luke xv there are expressed a life and thought out of the ordinary. Behind it and through it we see a conviction of God's love, not without parallel perhaps, but seldom if ever expressed with such clear and con-vincing power. The story was never copied from some commonplace book. It sprang from life, the

[1] Cf. *Lalita Vistara*, ch. xiii, Sacred Books of the East, xxi, p. 133.

life that is always felt through the teaching of Jesus, when men are great enough or simple enough to open their minds to it.

A particular example of such responsiveness may serve to illustrate and enforce the argument. Rather more than a year ago I received the following particulars in a letter from a friend returning to China on a P. & O. boat. "There is a very learned and interesting Japanese Professor from Tokio University on board, who speaks broken and quaint English. I have just found him reading a Japanese book and making marginal notes with his fountain pen copiously. On inquiry I found he was reading the New Testament, a version published by an American Press. He said that the Japanese language of the version was 'not very good': and when he cannot understand it, he checks off with a German Bible, which he carries in his pocket." My friend then reported some of the Japanese philosopher's impressions of Jesus. "Jesus speaks very free and glibly."..."His logic is about life. After him it became dogma. Modern logic is about the dead world."..."He sees things like the Japanese do." "Civilisation is not new.... He said he was the word in the beginning. Civilisation is not new. Material applications are new." "Jesus is very naïve. He is a source of light." Here is a Japanese scholar repeating the experience of Pascal when he said, "Jesus utters the deepest truths as if he had never had to think about them." The sense of life in the teaching of Jesus is irresistible and universal in its appeal. "He sees things like the Japanese do."

We shall be always indebted to the primitive Christian community from the midst of whose life the gospels came. But the life of that community was quickened and inspired by their Lord and Master. The Christ is not the projection of the church, the church is the creation of the Christ. At long last the disciples did not choose Him, but He chose them.

NOTE B

CHRIST-MYTH THEORIES AND SYNOPTIC CRITICISM

A very curious contribution to Synoptic criticism may be found on p. 166. "Perhaps (?) Kalthoff considers it possible that the two tales in the gospels concerning the faithless steward who 'makes to himself friends of the Mammon of unrighteousness' (Luke xvi. 1–9) and the sinful woman who is forgiven her sins, 'which are many: for she loved much' (Luke vii. 36–48) were included in the gospels in order 'to provide an ecclesiastical interpretation and sanction' for the dubious characters of Marcia and Callistus, who were so prominent in the Christian congregation at Rome. This may also serve as a contribution to the history of the origin of the gospels." Mr S. B. Slack, in a little volume on Early Christianity, also singles out this suggestion of Kalthoff for special praise. "The student who wishes for a temperate treatment of the life of Christ from the sceptical standpoint may read Kalthoff's *Entstehung des Christentums*. Kalthoff has done a service by calling attention to the fact that some parts of the New Testament appear to have originated on Italian (or Sicilian) ground. It may well be the case, for example, that the story in Luke vii. 37 f. was suggested by the conversion of Marcia, the concubine of the Emperor Commodus (180–192), or that the parable in Luke xvi. 1 f. may have been intended to justify the financial irregularities of Pope Callistus (about 220)." (*Early Christianity*, p. 31.) As it happens, both these stories are included in Tatian's *Diatessaron*, which certainly cannot be later than 180, and both are discussed in Tertullian's treatise against Marcion. The said treatise is written before the time of Callistus, and the presumption is that both stories stood in Marcion's text of Luke as early as 150. There is no reason to connect either story with Italian or Sicilian ground, and it is quite impossible that there should be any connection in either case with Marcia or Callistus. If this is the chief contribution of Kalthoff to the understanding of gospel origins, what can be the worth of his temperate reconstruction as a whole, and what are we to think of the critical judgment of Kautsky and Mr Slack who draw special attention to such irrelevant suggestions?

With the general failure of radical theories of Christian origins to obey the canons of scientific inquiry, I have dealt in a little book entitled *Rationalism and Historical Criticism*.

NOTE C

THE ESSENES

Kautsky's way of approach may be tested most easily by examining his account of the Essenes. "Like the Zealots, the Essenes were of proletarian origin, but quite different in character." This, in itself, is note-worthy. Different sections of the proletariat may react to the same economic situation in quite different ways. It follows that neither the economic situation nor the common class-interest or class-consciousness will ac-count for the emergence of two types of response. The Marxist will of course save his hypothesis by assuming endless subsidiary economic influences, past and pre-sent, but his system more and more resembles the Ptolemaic astronomy with its cycles and epicycles, and loses all that glamour of simplicity and finality which was its first attraction. Really the difference between Zealots and Essenes may have to be traced, not to special economic forces, but to different moral and religious beliefs.

We must, however, raise a previous question. Have we any right to describe the Essenes as of proletarian origin and to assume that their experiment in com-munism was an attempt to improve the economic situation of the proletariat? The answer is, we have no right whatever, for tradition tells us nothing on the subject. It is worth noting, though Kautsky does not note it, that the Therapeutae in Egypt, who in many respects resembled the Essenes, are described as "wealthy and well-born".[1] The Essenes may have been drawn from the same social rank. There is no reason to trace any connection between them and the

[1] Philo, *De Vita Contemplativa*, p. 109, Conybeare's edition.

city-proletariat. The Essenes probably do not represent a class-movement at all. Kautsky's assumption that communism must be associated with the proletariat is in itself untenable. Communist theories and aspirations are not peculiarly characteristic of proletarians, and few communist experiments have been purely or primarily proletarian in origin. Nor is there any reason for supposing that the Essenes adopted communism mainly as a solution of an economic problem. They appear to have adopted their way of life not to remedy the poverty of the proletariat, but to realise an ideal of holy living which was impossible in the troubled world of the Maccabean period. Kautsky is probably wrong even when he underlines the practical reasons which made the Essenes for the most part abandon marriage. "He who knows the history of communism will at once understand that it was not the nature of women, but the nature of the communistic household, that disgusted the Essenes with marriage."[1] This is highly dubious, if it suggests that the Essenes only came to abandon marriage through practical experience of the difficulties of monogamy in a communistic household. No analogy can be drawn from the history of other communistic societies, which reveal no general law. Some societies have prohibited marriage and some have adopted free-love, as a principle from the start. Probably every possible succession of no-marriage on ascetic principles, free-love, and monogamy has been tried in some communist society or other. The Essenes started with strict celibacy, because they held disparaging views of the nature of women, because they regarded family ties as antagonistic to the realisation of their

---

[1] *Foundations of Christianity*, p. 311.

communist ideal, and because sexual relations infringed their idea of purity. In spite of Kautsky, their hostility to marriage almost certainly was due in the first instance to an ascetic impulse.[1] Kautsky only asserts the contrary because he assumes that practical considerations arising out of economic organisation must be the real reasons determining men's conduct. This assumption rests on *a priori* theory, not on historical observation.

[1] On this point see Ginsburg, *The Essenes*, p. 39, n. 19.

Lecture III

THE GUIDING HAND OF GOD IN HISTORY

When the fulness of the time was come, God sent forth his Son, made of a woman, made under the law, to redeem them that were under the law, that we might receive the adoption of sons.

GAL. IV. 4, 5

A FAMOUS passage towards the close of New-man's *Apologia* describes, with a certain personal intensity, the difficulty of tracing God's providence in history. Strong in the testimony of conscience, Newman could not question the reality of God, but as soon as he sought to find God in the outside world and particularly in the realm of history, he felt dizzied and appalled. "If I looked into a mirror, and did not see my face, I should have the sort of feeling which actually comes upon me, when I look into this living busy world, and see no reflexion of its Creator....

"To consider the world in its length and breadth, its various history, the many races of man, their starts, their fortunes, their mutual alienation, their conflicts; and then their ways, habits, governments, forms of worship; their enterprises, their aimless courses, their random achievements and acquirements, the impotent conclusion of long-standing

facts, the tokens so faint and broken of a superintending design, the blind evolution of what turn
out to be great powers or truths, the progress of
things, as if from unreasoning elements, not towards final causes, the greatness and littleness of
man, his far-reaching aims, his short duration, the
curtain hung over his futurity, the disappoint-
ments of life, the defeat of good, the success of evil,
physical pain, mental anguish, the prevalence and
intensity of sin, the pervading idolatries, the cor-
ruptions, the dreary hopeless irreligion, that condition of the whole race, so fearfully yet exactly
described in the Apostle's words 'having no hope
and without God in the world'—all this is a vision
to dizzy and appal; and inflicts upon the mind
the sense of a profound mystery, which is absolutely
beyond human solution."[1]

Some of the very features of human experience
which Newman regarded as difficult might prove
on second thoughts to be confirmations of men's
faith in providence. "The blind evolution of what
turn out to be great powers and truths" may be
evidence that God leads the blind by a way they
know not, and "the progress of things, as if from
unreasoning elements, not towards final causes"
may bear witness to an unconscious teleology more
impressive in character than the natural order in

[1] *Apologia* (pocket edition, 1907), pp. 266, 267.

accordance with the best, which Socrates desired Anaxagoras to demonstrate. That the results which men actually achieve differ from the results they originally envisage may show God's tender mercies over all His works. The sentence of Joseph to his brethren, "So now it was not you that sent me hither, but God",[1] affirms God's victory through the aimless courses, aye, through the evil courses of men. The tokens of a superintending design may indeed be broken, but are they as faint and indistinct as Newman supposed?

In the coming of Jesus, if anywhere in history, we should find such tokens most evident and most convincing. When St Paul wrote that in the fulness of time God sent forth His Son, he may well have assumed that the fulness of time had come, since God had sent His Son. God never is before His time and never is too late. This is the language of faith: but we shall not be failing in either reverence or humility if we ask whether the insight of faith does not now find corroboration in the considered judgment of history.

In the light of our present knowledge of the ancient world, we may see a meaning in the fulness of time of which St Paul himself can hardly have been aware. The labours of a generation of scholars have made familiar to us the main trends of Hellenistic culture in the Augustan period, and we can

[1] Genesis xlv. 8.

gauge the nature of the appeal of Christianity more
accurately than Gibbon.

To St Paul, as to Dr Klausner, Greco-Roman
civilisation would appear as "a world decaying for
lack of God and social morality". If this is not
the whole truth and if the picture of society drawn
in the first chapter of Romans is one-sided, it is
true that alike in its conscious quests and in its
indifference, in its scepticism and in its weakness,
the ancient world was in desperate need of a religion and an ethic that should be at once universal
and personal. Society, if it was to be saved, required a faith and a moral standard which should
appeal to men as men and which individuals could
appropriate and make their own.

The conquests of Alexander introduced an age
of adventurers and self-made men, and began the
fusion of East and West in the Mediterranean
world. Old social ties were weakened. Old loyal-
ties, old ideals, bound up with the city-state, were
steadily undermined though not at once destroyed.
Cosmopolitanism and individualism are characteristic of the two centuries before Christ, and when
Augustus established his authority, the Roman
Empire functioned as a melting-pot somewhat after
the fashion of the United States to-day. The revival
of commerce in a now effectively policed world
tended to a mingling of races and nationalities with

w   6

far-reaching cultural reactions. Men had to learn to think of themselves as citizens of the world, to learn to say, in the phrase of Marcus Aurelius, "Dear city of Zeus", instead of "dear city of Cecrops". A world-wide empire required an inner bond of union, common social standards, a common religious faith.

We frequently hear references to the failure of nerve which characterised the ancient world. The rule of Augustus was welcomed as an escape from a situation which had become intolerable. The age of self-seeking adventurers produced such chaos, such perpetual conflict, such loss of life and such squandering of wealth that men turned with relief to an efficient despotism. For Romans the acceptance of the empire was a confession of failure. The Republic could not be made safe for the world, and the republican virtues could not be revived. Things had come to such a pass that throughout the provinces security was felt to be the highest good, and political liberties might well be exchanged for the suppression of bandits and freedom from civil war.

The sense of moral failure was very real. The well-known verse of Horace,

> Damnosa quid non imminuit dies?
> Aetas parentum peior avis tulit
> Nos nequiores, mox daturos
> Progeniem vitiosiorem.[1]

[1] *Odes*, Bk. III, Od. 6, l. 45 f. This is a kind of reversed Coué-ism. It might be rendered, "Every day and in every way we grow worse and worse".

is neither the conventional plaint of age against youth nor the wail of the *laudator temporis acti*. Again, it is not the expression of a philosophy of deterioration, an anticipation of Oswald Spengler. But like Spengler's philosophy, Horace's verse is the reflection of a generation laid waste morally by war.

Economic dependence on the institution of slavery co-operated with the surrender of political responsibility to Cæsar in producing a society marked by love of pleasure and lack of moral stamina. The tendency was to multiply the coarser pleasures and to give rein to pleasures not simply coarse but vicious. The whole moral tone of society was being steadily lowered by slavery.

When Horace describes his contemporaries as worse than their fathers, he may be suggesting intellectual deterioration as well as moral failure. There is at least some ground for asserting that the failure of nerve extended to men's trust in reason. That technical efficiency declined or at least stagnated, and that slavery itself would contribute to such decline, is true enough. But slavery may be symptom rather than main cause, and the movement of scientific thought which we owe to Greece began to slow down and eventually came to a halt for other reasons than technical inefficiency due to a slave-economy. The Romans themselves, like the

Marxists we may observe, were a practical people and not inclined to pursue scientific inquiries of which they could not perceive the immediate utility. The Greek tradition could be assimilated but not advanced by the Roman mind. And even before the advent of Rome to power, the schools of Alexandria seem to have entered upon the stage of reporting progress, of conserving and diffusing by education the cultural gains of the past instead of seeking to develop them further. However we account for it, the spirit of curiosity flagged at least in the realm of natural philosophy. Men lost confidence in the power of reason to discover truth and to answer their questions. In such a mood, old superstitions return and gain ground. Belief in demons and magic, belief in mascots and chance, belief in the influence of the stars and fate, revived and spread widely in the early Roman Empire. This sense of intellectual failure is also evidenced by increased respect for what is old. Wisdom to be trusted must be tried, and men looked for guidance to something that might claim to be the wisdom of the ages. Perhaps among Oriental peoples a wisdom might be found that antedated the traditions of Greece and Rome. The cult of Isis and Osiris might owe part of its authority to the fact that Egypt was old in civilisation when Greece was young.

The positive attempts to give the ethic and faith required are best represented in the Stoics and Epicureans. These schools of philosophy have this in common that they hold up ideals and suggest standards which might be acceptable to all men. They addressed themselves to Man, much as the eighteenth-century moralists did. A real analogy subsists between the humanitarianism of the eighteenth century and the humanitarianism of the Stoic and Epicurean. Charity towards the poor and humanity towards slaves would characterise both, but the eighteenth-century doctrines envisaged institutional reforms which the ancient philosophies did not entertain.

The Epicurean and Stoic alike set out to tell us how a man, any man, may live the good life. The theories of the former may be more suited to an exploiting or a leisured class, bent on consumption and enjoyment, though such an estimate does scant justice to Epicurus himself. We can trace even more clearly in the Cyrenaic philosophy, described by Walter Pater in *Marius the Epicurean*, the kind of principle by which the wealthier classes were apt to be guided in their search for the good life. To live for the most exquisite and refined sensation of the moment from moment to moment is the highest wisdom, and such wisdom has its admired exponents to-day. Stoicism appealed rather to those who, unlike the Epicureans, had still some sense of public duty, disillusioned and defeated as they often were. But whether with the Epicurean you are using reason to maximise pleasure or whether with the Stoic you are steeling yourself to be independent of all outward circumstances, the ideal you are pursuing is at once universal and individual.

The ancient world was also aware of the ineffectiveness of an abstract morality. Kautsky observes that "the more impotent the individual feels himself to be, the more timidly he seeks for a firm support in some personality that stands out from the ordinary average"—an observation the truth of which makes Kautsky's discounting of the personality of Jesus very difficult to justify. The development of the imperial cult was not something artificial enforced from above. It had its roots in this popular desire to find support, moral support, in some great man. In the case of Julius Cæsar, Kautsky notes, divine honours were accorded to him not by a mere resolution but by the inner conviction of the people. That the worship of the Emperor had much effect upon character is highly improbable, but hero-worship is commended as a source of moral strength in a well-known letter of Seneca. "We must", writes Seneca, "seek out some good man and keep him constantly

before our eyes, in order that we may so live and
act as though we were in his sight. So Epicurus
prescribed, giving us in this way a guardian and
a guide: and not without reason. Many sins are
suppressed if a witness comes on the scene before
the deed is done. Our heart must have someone
to honour, someone by whose example it may
consecrate its inner life. Happy is he who can
find such an one to venerate that he himself becomes moulded to the image which abides in his
memory! We need one by whose example our
morals may be formed: without a standard, what
is wrong will not be set right! (Ep. XI).... Clothe
thyself with the spirit of some great man and
separate thyself from the opinions of the multitude."

In the world of religion, men sought more
earnestly than ever for an assurance of another,
higher world and of one's share in it. Men were
afflicted both by a weariness of life and by the fear
of death. This world seemed less worth while but
the other world was still dark and unsure. Religious
beliefs were in chaotic confusion. The old theo-
logies were discredited but not discarded, and
monotheism, the unifying principle in religious life
and thought which was needed to match the
political unity of the Empire, was not so much
difficult to discern as difficult to establish.

Cicero's three books *De Natura Deorum* afford an interesting glimpse into the mind of educated Romans at the close of the Republican era. The Epicurean Velleius, the Stoic Balbus, and the Academic Cotta, are all alike unwilling to make a complete break with popular religion and traditional mythologies. The Epicurean indeed is anxious to get rid of divination, of the belief in fate, or in providence, "for who would not fear a God who looks after everything, thinks of everything, notices everything, a God who supposes that everything concerns Himself, a prying busybody?" Nevertheless we must believe that the gods exist, that they are eternal and that they are blessed or happy. They do not trouble themselves about us, but we should hold them in honour. It was suspected, and not without reason, that Epicurus only refrained from denying the gods outright for fear of shocking public opinion. If, however, his recognition of the gods was more deeply rooted (and it may well be that a philosopher who accepted the evidence of the senses so uncritically as Epicurus did could hardly dismiss the widespread belief in the actual appearance of gods and nymphs and other supernatural beings) it shows how difficult it was even for him to emancipate himself from popular religious beliefs. But when the Epicurean position is taken seriously, it breaks down under the

Academic criticism. These gods who do nothing have no claim on men's recognition or gratitude. "The Egyptians had better grounds for reverencing the ibis, a helpful bird. The barbarians regard some wild beasts as sacred because of services rendered. The gods of Epicurus not only do no service, but they do nothing whatever. This idea of the gods being perfectly happy because they have nothing to do is after all rather puerile. Epicurus, like pampered school boys, thinks nothing is better than a holiday. Yet boys themselves on holiday delight in some mirth-provoking occupation. But we want God on holiday to be so steeped in inaction that if He should move we fear lest He should be unable to be happy."[1] Presumably the gods lead a kind of Jack Horner existence, perpetually saying to themselves, if not "what good boys we are", then "what lucky devils we are". That is the drift of Book I, chapter 41, which is worth recalling. "But they have no pain, you say. Is that enough to constitute this supremely blessed life which overflows with good? God constantly reflects, we are told, having nothing else to occupy his thoughts, upon his blessedness. Picture then in your mind, and summon before your eyes

[1] Cicero, *De Natura Deorum*, bk. I, ch. 20, cc. 36 fin. and 37 init. I have adopted, with slight modifications, the vigorous translation by Mr Francis Brooks.

a God whose only reflection through all eternity is 'Capital berth this!' and 'Blessed am I!'... Now can there be anything supremely excellent in a nature which luxuriates in its own well being, and which never has performed, never does perform, and never will perform an action? And what piety is owed to a being from whom you have received nothing? What in fact can be owed at all to one from whom no benefit proceeds? Piety is right dealing towards the gods, but what question of right can there be between us and them, when man has no community with God? Holiness, again, consists in the knowledge of how to worship the gods, but why they should be worshipped when no good is either received or expected from them, I do not understand."

In more serious vein Cotta argues that Epicurus tears up religion by the roots when he denies that any help or favour comes to men from the gods. "But it was when he deprived the immortal gods of the attributes of help and benevolence that Epicurus tore religion from men's hearts by the roots. Although he says that the divine nature is supremely high and excellent, he nevertheless denies the existence of benevolence in God, taking away that which is the most essential characteristic of a supremely high and excellent nature, for there is nothing higher or more excellent than kindness and beneficence. When you assert that God does not possess this, you assert that no one, god or man, is dear to God, that no one is loved by him, and no one esteemed, from which it follows that the gods are not only regardless of men, but are in their own persons mutually regardless of one another."[1]

The Stoic is much more genuinely religious. He has more real sympathy with popular traditional religion and tries to do justice to old mythologies by rationalising and allegorising their details. His faith in God rests on the argument from design which had impressed philosophers ever since the regular movements of the heavens and heavenly bodies were observed. The providential ordering of the earth for man's benefit is proof of God's care for us, and man himself exhibits the wisdom and philanthropy of his maker. Man's sense of awe is stimulated by the more terrible aspects of nature, the earthquake and the thunderstorm for example, while his gratitude is stirred by presages of the future that come through oracles, auguries and dreams. For knowledge of the future is evidence of divine inspiration. The actual concept of the divine among the Stoics remains somewhat hazy. God is normally identified with Nature or with an *anima mundi*, a soul of the world hard to dis-

[1] Cicero, *De Natura Deorum*, I, 43.

tinguish from Nature, and then the Stoic verges towards the dark night of pantheism. But when he is allegorising myths the distinct attributes of the divine spirit shade off into the denizens of a polytheistic pantheon. His trend toward monotheism remains half-hearted.

For Cotta as for Velleius, the Stoic retains too much of popular superstition for rational defence. The ambiguities in the Stoic conception of God, the patent absurdities of their etymological clues to the meaning of old myths, the trivial character of the methods of augury and divination, as well as the trivial and sometimes misleading character of the knowledge of the future so disclosed, and lastly the problem of evil in all its aspects, make the Stoic position difficult for an educated man. Cotta would like to be a Stoic, and indeed out of reverence for his ancestral religion, he holds many of their conclusions; but he is not convinced by their arguments. As the first century advanced, it was not so much through Stoicism as through the mystery religions that many found the sense of the divine reality, the moral support and the assurance of immortality which they sought from religion and philosophy.

It is easy now to see how closely Christianity was related to the needs of the ancient world. That men needed to be assured of the unity of the divine requires no demonstration. But mere abstract monotheism is not enough. God must be true, not the prying busybody of whom the Epicureans were so anxious to get rid, and not the futile capricious deities of pagan mythology, but a God in whom men might put their trust. And God must be living, so real that all the half-gods go, and all the demons vanish. No intellectual scepticism, only faith in the living God, can release men from the bonds of superstition and fear. But he must be a god who acts and acts in mercy to mankind. It was this faith in God which the Christian missionaries spread through the Empire. Their faith was contagious, for as Edward White once put it, "if the Roman world believed nothing much, these men believed nothing doubting". And men turned from idols to serve the living and true God.

God's action in sending Jesus to be the Christ is the source of conviction. The Christ had to be interpreted to be the Saviour of the world, but Messianism had significance for the Gentile world, particularly in the evidence of the fulfilment of prophecy. Gibbon chides the early Greek apologists for parading the argument from prophecy. "When they demonstrate the divine origin of Christianity, they insist much more strongly on the predictions which announced than on the miracles which accompanied the appearance of the Messiah.

Their favourite argument might serve to edify a
Christian or convert a Jew, since both the one and
the other acknowledge the authority of those
prophecies and both are obliged, with devout
reverence, to search for their sense and their ac-
complishment. But this mode of persuasion loses
much of its weight and influence when it is addressed to those who neither understand nor respect the Mosaic dispensation and the prophetic
style."[1] In a footnote Gibbon refers readers to the
contempt expressed for the prophecies by Lucian
and Celsus, but in the case of the latter, Origen
acutely observes that the vehemence of his attack
on prophecies bears witness to their appeal. "From
these sentences it seems that Celsus felt the prophecies spoken of Jesus to be of great weight in
convincing hearers",[2] and there is no doubt that
the appeal of this argument was effective. The
Apologists were not as foolish as Gibbon supposed,
and the great historian himself is convicted of
sharing the eighteenth-century lack of perspective.
For the antiquity, often exaggerated by both Jews
and Christians, of the Old Testament writings in
itself made a profound impression. And the discovery of ancient prophecies fulfilled gave the evi-

---

[1] *Decline and Fall of the Roman Empire,* ed. Bury, vol. ii, p. 73
and note 194.
[2] *Contra Celsum,* vii, 14.

dence of divine inspiration which men sought so dubiously in oracle and augury. Intimations of future happenings, communicated through the exploration of the entrails of sacrificial animals, can scarcely compare with prevision through the mind and conscience of a prophet. Contrasted with the evidence of foreknowledge produced by Balbus from Roman history, the argument from prophecy was impressive and magnificent. God's action in fulfilling these detailed previsions in Christ's story was a miracle which outweighed as it included all the miracles that accompanied the incarnation.

Dr Claude Montefiore has finely said, Jesus took the treasures of Israel and made them available for mankind. For the Jews possessed the knowledge of God and His will, the knowledge needed by a world dying for lack of God and social morality. In a remarkable passage, Dr Klausner points out that Jesus detached these essentials from all the peculiarities which separated Jews from Gentile. This is indeed Klausner's complaint against Jesus. "Jesus came and thrust aside all the requirements of the national life: it was not that he set them apart and relegated them to their separate sphere in the life of the nation: he ignored them completely: in their stead he set up nothing but an ethico-religious system bound up with his conception of the Godhead.... In the self-same moment he both annulled Judaism as the life-force of the Jewish nation, and also the nation itself as a nation. For the religion which possesses only a certain conception of God and a morality acceptable to *all* mankind, does not belong to any special nation, and consciously or unconsciously breaks down the barriers of nationality. This inevitably brought it to pass that his people, Israel, rejected him."[1] Dr Klausner correctly interprets the difference between Christianity and Judaism and the reason for Israel's rejection of Jesus. But "a religion which possesses only a certain conception of God and a morality acceptable to all mankind" was precisely the religion of which the ancient world stood in need. It is hardly necessary to show in detail how the social morality of the Christian religion was related to the problems of the ancient world. The practice of infanticide and lax sexual conventions were the points at which Christianity challenged ancient society without compromise, just as the humanitarian outlook, embracing charity to the poor and humanity towards slaves, was the point at which the new religion reinforced what was best in the prevailing ethical philosophies of the time. And in the person of Jesus, men found the outstanding heroic figure by whose presence and influence morals

[1] Klausner, *Jesus of Nazareth*, p. 390, and cf. p. 376.

might be reformed. When St Paul wrote to his converts in Corinth, "Put ye on the Lord Jesus", he was probably not echoing Seneca, but the thought would appeal to all who felt their own impotence and their need of moral support.

If the coming of Jesus and the drastic simplification of Judaism for which Jesus was responsible seem peculiarly suited to the conditions of the Roman world, in what relation did Jesus stand to the situation of the Jewish people? The main feature of that situation and the nature of the people's reaction to it are admirably set forth in a sentence of Dr Klausner. "In its deeper consciousness, the nation felt that then more than at any other time, they must not be swallowed up in the great cauldron of nations in the Roman Empire, which were decaying for lack of God and social morality."[1] The dominant tendency was Pharisaic. Build a hedge round the Law, strengthen the barrier between Jew and Gentile, because only so can the treasures entrusted to Israel, the knowledge of God and of His will, be preserved for mankind. So argued devout Jewish patriots in the time of Jesus, and Dr Klausner holds that history has justified them. The crisis for Judaism was a profound and prolonged one. The Pharisaic way of meeting it, by faithful observance of the law

[1] *Loc. cit.*

and by waiting for God's deliverance guaranteed by a sign from heaven, won wide acceptance among the Jews, and still evokes our admiration to-day. Other solutions were sought by the Sadducees and Herodians, by the Zealots or their predecessors. The Sadducees would play for safety. Security by worldly wisdom and skilful diplomacy might well have been their slogan. The Herodians would seem to have expected to preserve Jewish nationality and develop Jewish independence by loyalty to the house of Herod. But more fiery patriots believed in more active measures. Heaven helps those who help themselves. Resist oppression, decline to pay iniquitous taxes to Rome, and God will prosper His people in arms. Stephen Liberty has suggested with considerable force that the Temptations of Jesus are related to the different reactions of sections of the Jewish people to the crisis in the life of the nation. In refusing to turn stones into bread, Jesus declines to play for safety with the Sadducee. In resisting the temptation to throw himself down from the Temple, Jesus disappoints the expectation of a sign from heaven entertained by the Pharisees. In declining the offer of the kingdoms of the world, Jesus rejects the way of the Zealot and of Judas the Gaulonite. If in Jesus was to be found the solution of the problem of the relation of the Jews to the Empire, the solution was not in accordance with the expectations or the wisdom of His contemporaries.[1]

But the crisis for the Jewish people was not merely outward, not merely a matter of their preservation from the perils of absorption in the cauldron of the Roman Empire. It was also inward, and arose from the unresolved tensions implicit in the development of the religion of Israel. The true nature of the problem which confronted the Jewish people is analysed in a masterly fashion by Professor C. H. Dodd in his book, *The Authority of the Bible*, and particularly in a chapter on "the inconclusiveness of the Old Testament religion". The Old Testament is admittedly an incomplete revelation. The religion of the Old Testament is a religion of hope, in that it expects a fuller and more perfect unfolding of God's will when Messiah comes or when God raises up a prophet like unto Moses. But Judaism is an attempt to systematise an incomplete revelation, and such attempts however worth while have their inevitable limitations. Dr C. H. Dodd writes, "there are evidences of strain and tension within the accepted system as various unsolved questions are brought into prominence by the pressure of changing conditions. Partly they are due to insufficient assimilation or application

[1] See *The Political Relations of Christ's Ministry*, by Stephen Liberty.

of prophetic ideas, partly to defects or gaps in the prophetic teaching itself".[1] Of the tensions which Professor Dodd proceeds to discuss we may put first the contradiction inherent in a national monotheism. The elements of universalism and nationalism are in conflict or in uneasy association in the Old Testament prophets. The universalism of Ruth and Jonah stands contrasted with the nationalism of Ezekiel and Ezra. If there is but one God, He must be God of the whole earth and of all peoples. Yet this one God is peculiarly the God of Israel, and if the knowledge of God be shared with other peoples, what becomes of Jewish nationality? The experience of the Jews as a people after the Exile had tended to emphasise the nationalism in their religion. The history of the Maccabees and the menace of Rome reinforced this side of the Old Testament religion.

The opposition, often latent rather than manifest, between cultus and the ethical spiritual religion of the prophets is another unresolved tension in Judaism. It is difficult even for a modern Jew to realise the part played by the old sacrificial system in the religion of his people in the time of Jesus. The destruction of the Temple tended to make Judaism more ethical and more spiritual,

[1] *The Authority of the Bible*, ch. VIII, p. 171. The whole chapter should be consulted.

in the prophetic sense, than it was before. At all times it is easy to overvalue religious duties, in the narrow technical sense of the term 'religious', i.e. duties connected with the routine of public worship. But for the first-century Jews this preoccupation with cultus and with the observance of personal religious rites and duties must have been particularly easy, since through it his devotion to God and his loyalty to his nation might find a satisfying expression. The sense of relative values given in the great prophets was not so readily retained. It was difficult for men in a religious system centring on the Temple at Jerusalem to realise with Hosea that God desires mercy and not sacrifice.

It may also be pointed out that the Temple-worship was not, as Kautsky suggests, simply a national vested interest. No doubt many besides the priests profited by this centralised form of worship. But for ordinary Jews it may well be, as Dr F. C. Grant suggests, that the ecclesiastical system was a financial burden which the orthodox Jew could not carry in addition to his ordinary secular taxation. Cultus presented an economic as well as a spiritual problem.

In all living religion there must be a tension, a healthy tension as von Hügel would say, between the transcendence and immanence of God. God is at once a god who is very far off and a god near at hand. If God were wholly other, He would, like the gods of Epicurus, tend to become unnecessary to human life. If God could be identified with the Stoic soul of the universe, or with our human best, He would not be God, since He would be subject to decay and could not be the source of inspiration and redemption. To resolve the tension in favour of one attribute to the exclusion of the other is always fatal alike in religion and philosophy. In the time of Jesus, there is much ground for thinking that God seemed to be remote and far-withdrawn. The emergence of the Scribe and the Rabbi in place of the prophet is some evidence of this. The development of apocalyptic in place of prophecy points in the same direction. The catastrophic character of the judgments and deliverances depicted in apocalyptic writings is itself proof that men could not find God at work in the world they knew. The growth of interest in angels among the less educated, and among the more educated the speculations about Wisdom as mediator between God and men, betray at once an awareness of a gulf between God and man and a desire to bridge it. The very Puritanism of the prophets made it difficult for ordinary folk to realise God's presence in daily life. That God is a god close at hand was a truth needing to be rediscovered.

Then, as Professor Dodd points out, the problem
of the sufferings of the righteous had received at
best but tentative solutions, and the facts seemed
to conflict with the prophetic theodicy, with the
prophet's confidence in the justice of God's judgments. I shall consider, in my next lecture, the
validity of the prophetic view of history. Here I
would only insist that alike in Job and Eccle-
siastes we can see that there were gaps in the
prophetic teaching. A kindred uncertainty attaches
to the hope of immortality as presented in the Old
Testament. Is there not something more to be
revealed concerning the souls of the righteous?
When we consider the situation of Judaism, external and internal, we can understand how men
looked and yearned for the fulfilment of God's
promise in the redemption of Israel.

That his followers regarded Jesus as the Messiah,
the Christ, is undeniable fact. That Jesus thought
of himself as the Messiah or at least as Messiah
designate, destined to be the Messiah, seems to me
to be almost as certain, in spite of the critical
doubts advanced by Wrede and renewed by Bultmann. The baptism of Jesus should be interpreted
as the dawn or confirmation of His Messianic
consciousness, and it is not rightly understood by
Mr Middleton Murry when he takes it as the expression of a filial consciousness meant to be normal

for mankind. The Temptation as recorded in the gospels is the temptation of the Messiah. This story Bultmann treats as a midrash, an episode imagined by some early Christian preacher and offered as an interpretation of the life of the Master, or to fill up a gap in the records. This theory seems to me rather arbitrary, especially as there is no suggestion of a temptation of the Messiah in previous anticipations of His coming and as there was no obvious gap in the records asking to be filled. If it be midrash, the writer had a singular insight into the principles by which Jesus was guided in His public ministry, and into the situation in Palestine at the time. The chapter on the Temptation in Seeley's *Ecce Homo* and Stephen Liberty's *Political Relations of Christ's Ministry* make this intimate connection of the Temptation story with the main features of the gospel narrative abundantly clear. And the Messianic consciousness present from the beginning of the public ministry implies that Israel is to be saved through Jesus.

Did then the teaching of Jesus offer any direct and conscious solution of the problems of Jewry and of Greco-Roman society? Was Jesus Himself fully aware either of the political relations of His ministry or of the relevance of His gospel to the needs of the Mediterranean world? Of conditions among the Gentiles Jesus would seem to have known little, and the wider world was very much on the periphora of His interests. If He transformed Judaism into a universal religion, He certainly did not make a deliberate transformation. He did not consciously adapt Judaism to Gentile needs.

Of the crisis in Israel He was clearly much more fully aware. The gospels, particularly the gospel of Luke, indicate a vivid sense of crisis. The warning that all might perish even as the Galileans whose blood Pilate mingled with their sacrifices, the parable of the barren fig-tree, the anticipation of judgment on the cities which had been the scene of his ministry, and likewise of the destruction of Jerusalem, all suggest awareness of the national peril. And clearly Jesus believed that the nation would escape or incur this judgment according as they received or rejected His message. How Jesus would have acted, if the people had recognised Him as Messiah, and what solution He would have found or at least sought for the problem of the relation of the Jews to the Roman Empire, we can only conjecture. But we may be confident that His way of meeting the peril would have been different from that of the Pharisees. He would have encouraged His people to risk their national identity, their life as a people in order to save it, in order to give to that Gentile world the faith and morality which it needed.

It is difficult to judge how far Jesus was aware of the unresolved tensions in Judaism and set out consciously to resolve them, or how far He recognised gaps in the prophetic teaching and set out deliberately to fill them. His teaching appears to spring spontaneously from His life with God, and He drew from the Old Testament and the tradition of His people all those positive truths which served to sustain His communion with His Father or which were endorsed by that inner life; but He does not underline the implications of His assertions or put a critical edge on His sayings. He does not attack Judaism as a system, though He denounces Rabbis or groups of Rabbis. Dr Claude Montefiore is puzzled that Jesus enunciates the precept, Love your enemies, but nowhere says in so many words, You, Jews, must love your enemies, the Romans. This in itself makes it clear that the teaching from the Sermon on the Mount was not prompted primarily by reflection on the needs of the international situation. It sprang out of the conviction of Jesus regarding the nature of God. When Jesus uttered the great truth, "nothing from without defileth a man", Dr Montefiore observes that He speaks like Amos or Isaiah. It is a great prophetic utterance. But it is the evangelist who notes, "*This he said*, making all meats clean", and Jesus Himself seems hardly to be aware that

He is abrogating whole sections of Leviticus. He was not deliberately breaking down the barrier between Jew and Gentile, and yet He has actually done it. Jesus does not appear to deal directly with the issues which we can discern. Yet the inner tensions of Judaism were resolved and the fundamental spiritual needs of the ancient world were met by the teaching of Jesus, which was at once a simplification and an enrichment of Judaism. The wavering uncertainties of Old Testament religion regarding the sufferings of the righteous and the hope of resurrection were confronted with the tremendous facts of Christ's death and resurrection. The history of Jesus became the basis of new religious convictions.

To bring new life and courage to a morally defeated world and to make the treasures of Israel available for mankind, Jesus had to die. Gethsemane suggests that the nature of the necessity of His death may not have been fully clear to Jesus Himself. Yet looking back, we can see that nothing but the Cross could break down the barrier between Jew and Gentile. Here the experience of St Paul is of decisive importance. He could see that if we say with the centurion, "Truly this was a righteous man", there must be something wrong with the zeal for the law that put Him to death. It was their devotion to their national faith which led the Jews to reject Jesus. It follows that for everyone who puts his trust in Christ, Christ is the end of law. The old legal religion is shown to be incapable of making men righteous. It is not thus that men come to know God and His will. So through the Cross one Pharisee came to pour contempt on all his pride, and realised that Jew and Gentile might enter into fellowship with one another and with God, without the yoke of the law. Is it going too far to say that we should not be thinking about Christianity to-day, we should not in any degree have been a Christian nation, if Jesus had not died and thereby smashed Judaism as a system, and if St Paul had not seen at least this meaning in His death? Of the assurance of forgiveness which men have found through the Cross, and of the consequent breaking of barriers of indifference and pride, of fear and guilt between men and God, I must not now speak. I would only insist that in the ministry and teaching, the death and resurrection of Jesus and in the close but far from fully conscious relation of the gospel to the problems of the ancient world, it is difficult to deny God's overruling Providence. "To all appearances, both individuals and groups carry out purposes of which they are only partly conscious."[1]

[1] Inge, *God and the Astronomers*, p. 252. Cf. P. Volz, *Mose und sein Werk*, p. 15: "The genius of Moses brought to light new discoveries of a unique character, demands whose bearing was not fully understood by himself". Something similar may be true of Jesus.

This was true, I believe, even of our Lord Himself. His appearing when and as He did was surely of God's ordering. It was God who sent His Son, in the fulness of time, to live under the law so as to release men from bondage to the law and make sonship possible for Jew and Gentile alike. "God was in Christ reconciling the world unto Himself."

Lecture IV

THE PROPHETIC INTERPRETATION
OF HISTORY

He that is not with me is against me; and he that gathereth not
with me scattereth abroad.   MATT. XII. 30

Seest thou these great buildings? There shall not be left here
one stone upon another, which shall not be thrown down.
                                               MARK XIII. 2

If thou hadst known, even thou, at least in this thy day, the things
which belong unto thy peace! but now they are hid from thine
eyes.   LUKE XIX. 42

THE prophet is distinguished from his fellows
by the strength of his moral conviction. His
moral insight is quickened by his religious
experience, and he perceives with a painful clear-
ness the connection between sin and its consequences. The prophetic outlook may vary in
character from the general belief in some connection between wrongdoing and disaster, to a
definite judgment as to the association of some
particular disaster with some particular wrongdoing. The judgment of the prophet may err either
in his assessments of right and wrong or in his view
of particular events. But to convict the prophet
of error in detail, even in important detail, does
not of itself suffice to deny the validity of the mode

of interpreting history which prophecy represents. For the prophet, history is the scene of moral judgments. Does the study of history confirm this reading of the past? Years ago Froude wrote in an address on "The Science of History": "One lesson and only one history may be said to repeat with distinctness: that the world is built somehow on moral foundations: that in the long run it is well with the good: in the long run it is ill with the wicked. But this is no science: it is no more than the old doctrine taught long ago by the Hebrew prophets".[1] Was Froude justified in claiming the support of history for the outlook of the Hebrew prophets, or was he merely, as Mr Butterfield would seem to suggest, anticipating the whig prejudice of Lord Acton?

Great historians and great philosophers have joined forces to warn the moralist off the field of history. Bury preferred Thucydides to Tacitus, because the former in making reflections of his own "never takes justice or morality into account, from which we may infer that in his estimation these conceptions did not illuminate the subject".[2] Tacitus, on the other hand, "like Sallust looked at history from an ethical point of view.... He judged actions by the ideals of virtue and nobility:

[1] *Short Studies in Great Subjects*, First Series, p. 21.
[2] *Ancient Historians*, p. 137.

he was not prepared to take time and circumstances into account nor to acknowledge that the standard applied to private conduct may be inapplicable to public transactions. In this respect he occupied the same ground as the late Lord Acton, whose first principle in reading history was the application of the strictest rules of private morality to the actions of public men. It may be thought by some that this attitude in examining the past is somewhat futile. Sociology is still in its infancy, and it may be asked, Has the time come for verdicts?"[1]

Hegel is numbered among those who condemn this attitude as futile. For him, world-historical men would seem to be beyond criticism and the saying 'Weltgeschichte ist Weltgericht' is tantamount to the view that whatever is, is right or, at least, is justified as a moment in a process of historical necessity. "What pedagogue has not demonstrated of Alexander the Great or of Julius Caesar that they were instigated by such passions [as a morbid craving for conquest] and were consequently immoral men? whence the conclusion immediately follows that he, the pedagogue, is a better man than they, because he has not such passions."[2] "For the great World-historical form

---

[1] *Op. cit.* pp. 231–2.
[2] *Philosophy of History*, p. 33 (Bohn edition).

of Alexander, the modern standard applied by recent historical 'Philistines'—that of virtue or morality—will by no means suffice."[1] Mr Butterfield echoes these sentiments of Bury and Hegel when in a chapter on "Moral Judgments in History" he refers to "the most useless and unproductive of all forms of reflection—the dispensing of moral judgments upon people or upon actions in retrospect".[2] Is the prophet to be dismissed in this way along with the pedagogue and the petit-bourgeois Philistine?

I believe myself that there is a good deal of confusion of thought in the discussion of this very important subject. On three points, the view which I understand to be represented by Bury and Hegel, and which is expounded at length by Mr Butterfield, appears to be substantially correct. In the first place, greatness in history cannot be equated with goodness, at least not with goodness as estimated by some narrow moral standard. The historian's first concern is with intrinsic greatness, and with significance in history.[3] He cannot measure greatness by some purely moral standard. Napoleon is amoral, consciously amoral, but Lord Acton who is supposed to have no eye save for

[1] *Op. cit.* p. 285.
[2] *The Whig Interpretation of History*, p. 108.
[3] Cf. an article by W. G. de Burgh on "Greatness and Goodness", *Proceedings of the Aristotelian Society*, N.S. vol. XXXII.

moral failings describes him as "the most splendid genius that has appeared on earth".[1] If we turn to the historical books of the Old Testament, which are written from a prophetic standpoint, then manifestly the kings of Israel are judged ungenerously. "Jeroboam son of Nebat who made Israel to sin" was historically a great person and possibly a better ruler than the book of Kings suggests. Secondly, the desire to reach definite black and white judgments on individuals and events may be very misleading and involve the moralist himself in untruth and injustice. Here again the convenience which we found as schoolboys in classifying the kings of Israel and Judah as good or bad, A 1 or C 3, is a sign that history has been oversimplified. Mr Butterfield's main polemic against the Whig interpretation of history really turns on this issue. At the very beginning of his book, he repudiates "any division of mankind into good and evil, progressive and reactionary, black and white".[2] He protests against an interpretation of history which traces through the ages "the working of an obvious principle of progress, of which the Protestants and whigs have been the perennial allies, while Catholics and tories have perpetually formed obstruction."[3] "Behind all the fallacies of the whig historian there lies the passionate desire

[1] *Historical Essays*, p. 458.   [2] *Op. cit.* p. 1.   [3] P. 12.

to come to a judgment of values, to make history answer questions and decide issues and to give the historian the last word in a controversy. He imagines that he is inconclusive unless he can give a verdict; and studying Protestant and Catholic in the sixteenth century he feels that loose threads are still left hanging unless he can show which party was in the right."[1] To approach history with the assumption that men can be classified as saints and sinners will certainly be disastrous. In the third place, Mr Butterfield is probably right as against Lord Acton, when he contends that the function of the historian is to act not as judge, but as expert witness. His business is to tell us what happened, without fear and favour. He has to see that we are put in possession of the relevant data. It is no part of his duty to dictate a final judgment to us. But the historian may still be described as 'the arbiter of controversies' because as an expert witness he is summoned to give evidence on the whole case and not for one side. And, one may add, if in the estimation of Thucydides and Bury, the conceptions of morality and justice do not illuminate the study of history, the study of history may still illuminate those conceptions.

It does not follow from all this that the historian can dispense with moral standards or refrain from

[1] Pp. 64–5.

moral judgments: still less does it follow that history has discredited the prophet. As Mr Butterfield himself reminds us, "We go to the past to discover not facts only but significances".[1] There are no bare facts for the historian. He has to deal with a world in which fact and value are inseparable. That is why the historian's equipment must exceed that of the natural scientist, and also why the moral discipline of historical research should be more searching than the moral discipline of observation and experiment in a physics laboratory. To quote Mr Butterfield again, "It is necessary that we should go with instinct and sympathy alive and all our humanity awake. It is necessary that we should call up from the resources of our nature all the things which deflect the thought of the scientist but combine to enrich the poet's".[2] Consequently the historian cannot be blind to moral values. He has at once to judge the past by the moral standards he accepts, and he has also to submit those moral standards themselves to the test of past experience. It is from the historian as expert witness that we must learn what moral standards have been accepted by societies in the past, and how far such standards have been practically effective. The historian must tell us when, how, and why these moral standards have been

[1] P. 93.   [2] P. 93.

changed. The historian must reveal the actual consequences, good or evil, of departures from or of adherence to these standards. A historian who ignores moral valuations cannot serve even as a witness. An expert witness must know what he is talking about. All this Mr Butterfield would admit, though he does not seem to realise the full significance of his admissions.

If he did appreciate the position of the historian as expert witness he would not countenance the view, often mistakenly adopted by historians, that history reduces us to pure relativism in morals or in any other realm of values. The office of history, according to Mr Butterfield, is "to show us that all our judgments are merely relative to time and circumstance".[1] In that sentence, the adverb 'merely' is quite indefensible. If it be pressed, we are back at "the doctrine that the whole realm of historical events is of no significance whatever",[2] a doctrine which Mr Butterfield elsewhere repudiates. For it is the essential paradox of our being involved in the process of history that all our judgments are necessarily relative, and yet all would be meaningless if they did not imply standards of value that transcend our present time and circumstance. The creative character of the acts that determine the historical process would be

[1] P. 75.   [2] P. 57.

impossible if all our judgments were *merely* relative
to time and circumstance.

When Mr Butterfield puts the historian in his
proper place and confines him to the task of reporting that "a thing is good or harmful according
to circumstances, according to the interactions
that are produced",[1] at least the standards of
goodness or harmfulness cannot be purely sub-
jective or relative, nor can they vary from age to
age. Wars and disasters and economic ruin are
objective enough, and if a theory or an institution
can be shown to produce disastrous interactions,
presumably history witnesses to some defect in
that theory or institution. Throughout his book,
Mr Butterfield confuses objectively valid moral
judgments with sweeping indiscriminate verdicts
and argues that moral judgments are not objectively valid because sweeping verdicts are usually
unjust and mistaken. "We can never assert that
history has proved any man right in the long run.
We can never say that the ultimate issue, the suc-
ceeding course of events, or the lapse of time have
proved that Luther was right against the Pope,
or that Pitt was wrong against Charles James
Fox."[2] That history does not permit us to say
that Luther was entirely right and the Pope entirely wrong, or even that Luther on the whole

[1] P. 75.   [2] P. 75.

was right and the Pope on the whole was wrong,
does not mean that we can form and express no
valid judgments about either. Is it impossible for
the historian to assert that Luther was definitely
right or definitely wrong in this action or that,
because we may hesitate to pronounce a verdict
on Luther's career and influence as a whole? Whatever our estimate of Luther's influence in general,
Luther at the Diet of Worms is a heroic world-
historic figure, and the stand he took then exerts
a continuous influence on the side of recognising
the freedom and the responsibility of the individual
conscience. To assert this is not to surrender to
whig prejudice, but to record the actual objective
significance of the event. Or take the case of
Charles James Fox. Must not the historian in the
light of modern research into the circumstances of
the taking of the Bastille declare that Fox was
quite definitely deceived and mistaken in the enthusiasm with which he greeted that event?[1]
Mr Butterfield deprecates taking sides in old dis-
sensions. "Studying the quarrels of an ancient day
(the historian) can at least seek to understand
both parties to the struggle and he must want to
understand them better than they understood
themselves; watching them entangled in the net
of time and circumstance he can take pity on

[1] Cf. Louis Madelin, *The French Revolution*, pp. 76–80.

them—these men who perhaps had no pity for
one another; and, though he can never be perfect,
it is difficult to see why he should aspire to anything less than taking these men and their quarrels
into a world where everything is understood and
all sins are forgiven."[1] But one cannot help asking
whether the only alternatives are violent partisan-
ship or something like a sentimental reconciliation? And after all, neither understanding nor
forgiveness is possible, apart from a sound moral
judgment. To forgive sin, you must be able to
recognise it as sin. The historian must not set out
to show which party was in the right, but he
should try to show how far each party was in the
right.

When Mr Butterfield says "we are deceived if
we deny that when Luther rebelled against the
Catholic Church, and the Popes so deliberately
hounded him into rebellion, they did not between
them produce a tragedy which meant the sacrifice
of more than one generation",[2] he does not apparently realise that he is committing himself to a
series of value-judgments as surely as any of the
besotted partisan historians whom he dubs whigs.
He may refrain from determining the relative
degrees of responsibility, but he manifestly condemns both the truculence of Luther and the

[1] P. 3.					[2] P. 89.

overbearing conduct of the Popes, and when he uses the word 'tragedy' he implies that we are in the presence of a conflict in which elements of nobility and greatness may be found on both sides. The difference between Mr Butterfield and the whig historians whom he castigates is not that they pass moral judgments and he does not, but that his moral judgments are more refined and more equitable than theirs. Thus to refine conscience is not to destroy but to confirm its authority.

The lessons to be drawn from history can hardly be confined to the verdicts of 'non-proven' permissible in Scottish murder trials. Even Hegel's saying that the only lesson we learn from history is that men do not learn from history, would lose its point if there were not other lessons which could and should be learnt from history. Such lessons might be only negative as Henry Sidgwick once suggested. History labels blind alleys and warns men against seductive short-cuts which have proved over and over again to be culs-de-sac. Or again we may say, as we have already admitted, that the lessons of history have no finality, but possess only varying degrees of probability. Yet the probability may be so clear and so strong that we neglect it at our peril. And if there are moral lessons or warnings to be found in history, this involves the assumption that events might have been other than they actually were. All moral judgments are futile if history is governed by necessity, whether that necessity be physical or psychical or logical. Over against the prophetic view of history stands the view that everything in the past is justified on the ground of necessity. Against such a canonisation of the past Lord Acton warned us in his inaugural lecture as Regius Professor of History. The view of history advocated in that lecture "deems the canonisation of the historic past more perilous than ignorance or denial, because it would perpetuate the reign of sin and acknowledge the sovereignty of wrong".[1] Mr Butterfield regards this very warning as one more proof of the thorough whig bias pervading Lord Acton's view of history. I cannot myself discern in Lord Acton's view the latent whig bias which seems so obvious to Mr Butterfield. The opposing view is certainly not tory. It is summarised by Lord Acton in the following terms. "For we have a theory which justifies Providence by the event, and holds nothing so deserving as success, to which there can be no victory in a bad cause; prescription and duration legitimate; and whatever exists is right and reasonable; and as God manifests His will by that which He tolerates, we must conform to the divine decree by living to shape the future after the ratified

[1] Cited in *The Whig Interpretation of History*, p. 110.

image of the past."[1] The authorities quoted in illustration of the theory are the philosopher, Leibniz, and the author of a Catholic Philosophy of History. The examples given of failure to maintain moral standards are Ranke's estimate of William III and Macaulay's characterisation of Halifax. It is precisely whig bias which Lord Acton was condemning when he warned us not to canonise the past. Mr Butterfield himself does not maintain the theory which Lord Acton condemns, and he actually confirms in large measure the theory which Lord Acton upholds.[2]

Anyone who recognises an element of tragedy in history is dealing with a moral order—not indeed the simple moral order embodied in the principle of Karma, but still an order essentially moral, if strange and mysterious. If ignorance, prejudice and sin produce disaster the evidence must be apparent in history. To Froude's mind at least the

---

[1] *Lectures on Modern History*, p. 25.
[2] Incidentally, Lord Acton is the only historian mentioned by name in Mr Butterfield's book as exemplifying the whig interpretation of history. Very few of the judgments attributed to whig historians would have been endorsed by Lord Acton and many of Mr Butterfield's own judgments might have been Lord Acton's. Thus the whig historian who, impressed by benefits attributed to the Reformation or to the Revolution of 1688, is tempted to forget the sufferings of a generation, and to assert that the original tragedy was no tragedy at all, would have found short shrift from Lord Acton. Such an historian is 'perpetuating the reign of sin' and 'acknowledging the sovereignty of wrong'.

evidence was clear. "(History) is a voice for ever sounding across the centuries the laws of right and wrong. Opinions alter, manners change, creeds rise and fall, but the moral law is written on the tablets of eternity. For every false word or unrighteous deed, for cruelty and oppression, for lust or vanity, the price has to be paid at last: not always by the chief offenders, but paid by some one. Justice and truth alone endure and live. Injustice and falsehood may be long-lived, but doomsday comes at last to them, in French Revolutions and other terrible ways."[1] This paragraph drew from John Morley a terrific rejoinder which Mr F. W. Hirst has summarised in the *Early Life and Letters of John Morley*. "Is it true", Morley asks, "that History is a voice for ever sounding across the centuries the laws of right and wrong; that for all cruelty and oppression, lust and vanity, the price has to be paid at last; that justice and truth alone endure? If so, we shall first of all have to revise our conceptions of justice, so as to include among its triumphs the punishment of children for the sins of their forbears, as when innocent Louis XVI was decapitated for the wickedness of Louis XV, the lust of the Regent, and the vanity of Louis XIV. Or, if we turn from the kings to nations, look at England and Ireland. England

---

[1] *Short Studies in Great Subjects*, First Series, p. 27.

conquered, and for centuries misgoverned, Ireland. Who suffered most?—the English, or the Irish? Surely the Irish. Take the rebellion of 1798, for instance, and see whether the guilty oppressors or the oppressed paid the price. 'England was barely scratched. Ireland was deluged with the blood of her own children. This may be the justice of history; it is not ethical justice.'

"Surely when we reflect on these things, the voice which comes to us across the centuries is not the paean of triumphant right and justice, but 'a doleful song, steaming up, a lamentation, an ancient tale of wrong'. If we look back into history as a great field of moral government, where punishment has been meted out to kings and peoples in nice proportion to their crimes, and prosperity and peace in nice proportion to their sufferings and their deserts, we find not justice and judgment, but a supreme chaos, a dizzy and unfathomable abyss.... The only penalty which we can with certainty pronounce against the unjust nation or man lies in the fact of injustice. To be corrupt and selfish, oppressive and lawless, is its own punishment. The only fixed law of retribution is that of the emphatic and final sentence: he that is unjust let him be unjust still, and he which is filthy let him be filthy still."[1]

[1] *Early Life and Letters of John Morley*, vol. I, pp. 82–3.

When we survey afresh this controversy between Froude and Morley, it is apparent that they were not so far apart as Morley supposed. Froude seems to have had a kind of gift for being misunderstood, and Morley in his haste overlooked the qualifications which Froude attached to the thesis he refutes. Froude says expressly that the price to be paid for injustice has to be paid by some one, not necessarily by the chief offenders. Froude is not asserting that history is administered by a humane Mikado or that it resembles some ideal court of law in which every criminal receives exactly the punishment he deserves. Both Froude and Morley deny that any exact system of retributive justice can be discerned in history and both assert the reality of vicarious suffering. The innocent and the less guilty suffer with and for the guilty. But Froude maintains that evil acquiesced in brings its penalty in the long run. This, seemingly, Morley questions or denies, but it is difficult to see on what grounds he bases his doubt or denial. It is not true that "the only fixed law of retribution is that of the emphatic and final sentence: he that is unjust let him be unjust still and he which is filthy let him be filthy still". In individual experience vice may be its own and its only punishment, but in history disaster sets limits to the multiplication of filth and injustice. Sooner or later the price has to be paid, in catastrophe and degradation, in world-wars and revolutions, when, as the Psalmist says, God answers us in terrible things but in righteousness. That there are chastisements in history and that men learn from them, is suggested by Mr Butterfield in an admirable paragraph. "When the sins and errors of an age have made the world impossible to live in, the next generation, seeking to make life tolerable again, may be able to find no way save by the surrender of cherished ideals, and so may find themselves compelled to cast about for new dreams and purposes. An important aspect of the historical process is the work of the new generation for ever playing providence over even the disasters of the old, and being driven to something like a creative act for the very reason that life on the old terms has become impossible." [1]

Whether a new generation makes a new start depends on something more than physical survival. The work of the new generation has to be creative and is not dictated by necessity. If a new generation is to play providence its success will depend on its moral stamina, on its faith, on its power to read the lessons of the past and the signs of the times. Moral judgments on the past, recognition of sin and error become essential elements of progress. The creative act requires prophetic insight.

[1] *Op. cit.* p. 77. Cf. also pp. 88, 89.

The history of the Jews provides the most striking instance of the survival of a people through faith. Disraeli's famous answer to the question concerning proof of the reality of God was neither flippant nor impertinent. The Jews have survived as a nation not through faith in themselves but through trust in God. Loisy has legitimately appealed to their example, as proof that not disaster in itself but the spirit in which a community faces disaster is the factor making history. "It is not in external conditions that the actual principle of social evolution resides, in so far as it is social and moral. Social evolution consists in society either controlling its external conditions morally or submitting to them to the loss of its morality. . . . We have even been able to see one people, the Jewish people, maintain themselves through disasters unparalleled, through persecution and oppression, in virtue of a national consciousness which was definitely religious and of a social discipline which was essentially moral. This people has thus lived by a fully conscious faith and a morality sincerely embraced. The example is unique: it is none the less instructive."[1]

Positively, the prophetic interpretation of history insists that only righteousness exalteth a nation, and that the just can live only by faith. Nega-

[1] Loisy, *La Morale Humaine*, pp. 120, 121,

tively, it asserts the awful consequences that flow
from ignorance and sin. "Except ye repent, ye
shall all likewise perish." "If thou hadst known
the things belonging to thy peace." In this connection, it must be remembered that the mills of
God grind slowly, that the consequences may be
long delayed. Morley treats this delay as the denial
of ethical justice. St Paul would interpret it as the
long-suffering patience of God calling men to repentance. For sin and disaster are not linked in
an automatic mechanical sequence, though the
connection is real and essential. Prophetic anticipations of disaster are always hypothetical judgments. 'Except ye repent' is the expressed or implied qualification.

The historian must perpetually remind himself
of the long run. To arm conscience, he must put
us on our guard against the glamour of immediate
success or prosperity. As an instance of what seems
to me a short-range historical judgment, I might
cite Lord Bryce's reliance on the history of the rise
of Prussia as proof that war is not incompatible with
progress. "The capital instance of the association
of war with the growth and greatness of a state
is found in Prussia. One may say that her history
is the source of the whole thesis and the basis of
the whole argument. It is a case of what, in the
days when I learned logic at the University of

Oxford, we used to call the induction from a single instance.... Three successful wars—those of '64, '66, '70–71—made Prussia the nucleus of a united German nation and the leading military power of the Old World.

"Ever since these victories her industrial production, her commerce, and her wealth have rapidly increased, while at the same time scientific research has been prosecuted with the greatest vigour and on a scale unprecedentedly large. These things were no doubt achieved during a peace of forty-three years. But it was what one may call a belligerent peace, full of thoughts of war and preparations for war. There is no denying that the national spirit has been carried to a high point of pride, energy and self-confidence, which have stimulated effort in all directions and secured extraordinary efficiency in civil as well as in military administration. Here then is an instance in which a state has grown by war and a people has been energised by war."[1]

This passage is the more remarkable because it is taken from an address in war time. Bryce, to his honour be it recorded, even in 1918 could survey thus dispassionately the rise of Prussia. He hastened to point out that war at best only in-

[1] Bryce on "War and Progress", *Essays and Addresses in Wartime*, 1918.

creases wealth and power, but with the proof
written in letters of blood before his eyes he failed
to observe that the illusion of military success and
the very pride it fosters were actually destroying
the wealth and power such victories had helped
to create. An historian with prophetic insight
would pass a different judgment from that of
Bryce. We are still discussing the causes of the
Great War as if they involved some obscure mystery.
The underlying moral cause is clear enough. Those
three successful wars, and the apparent triumph
of Bismarck's real-politik, deceived men into denying the claims of morality in international
politics. The standards of honesty expected of
private individuals, it was supposed, do not apply
to public actions. So far from its being the wisdom
of the scientific historian to make an essential distinction between private and public morality, as
Bury suggested, or at least to suspend judgment
on this question until sociology, of all sciences, has
come to some conclusion, it is the duty of the
historian to draw attention to the fact that wherever men have persistently ignored the moral order
in public affairs, they have been overtaken by
disaster. J. W. Headlam, writing in 1899 simply as
an historian, exposed the ominous outcome of the
weaknesses of Bismarck's character. On his retire-
ment, the old pilot criticised the Government un-

generously and exalted himself unduly. The effect on German public opinion was not confined to the weakening of the prestige of the Government. "More than this, he was attempting to destroy the confidence of the people in the moral justice and necessity of the measures by which he had founded the Empire. They had always been taught that in 1870 their country had been the object of a treacherous and unprovoked attack. Bismarck, who was always living over again the great scenes in which he had been the leading actor, boasted that but for him there would never have been a war with France. He referred to the alteration in the Ems telegram, which we have already narrated, and the Government was forced to publish the original documents. The conclusions drawn from these disclosures and others which followed were exaggerated, but the naïve and simple belief of the people was irretrievably destroyed. Where they had been taught to see the will of God, they found only the machinations of the Minister. In a country where patriotism had already taken the place of religion, the last illusion had been dispelled; almost the last barrier was broken down which stood between the nation and moral scepticism."[1]

[1] *Bismarck*, p. 460. Cf. also R. B. Mowat, *Public and Private Morality*, esp. p. 77.

If I may judge from Mr Butterfield's handling of the Spanish Inquisition which the historian, I gather, must regard as good during the struggle for national unity when it is claimed that the Inquisition increased the power and prestige of the nation, but which the historian will condemn as evil in so far as it contributed later on to the decadence of Spain, Bismarck's character and policy must likewise be pronounced good in the circumstances of 1870 but bad in the circumstances of 1914. I do not, however, believe that the historian can rightly limit himself to such piecemeal judgments. He cannot say that the Inquisition and real-politik are neither good nor bad in themselves, but good or bad as circumstances vary. Least of all can he adopt such an attitude if the institution or policy under consideration has an inherent tendency to create the circumstances in which it is proved and seen to be evil. It is part of the historian's task to keep in view long-period results and not to be duped by short-period successes. When one realises what idolising Bismarck has cost Europe, one suspects that to exempt world-historic figures from moral criticism in the spirit of Hegel is a disastrous mistake. Froude, Lord Acton, and the prophets are closer to the realities of history than Bury, Hegel and Mr Butterfield.

Prophetic authority has often been claimed for inadequate moral standards. The bloody assassinations carried out by Jehu at Jezreel are approved by the writer of II Kings. "The Eternal said to Jehu, 'Since you have done well in carrying out my will, punishing the house of Ahab, exactly as I intended, your sons shall sit on the throne of Israel down to the fourth generation'."[1] From the following verses the writer's standard was clearly the purity of public worship. In so far as Jehu stood for Jahweh against Baal he was doing God's will and his crimes became virtues. When he associated the worship of Jahweh with the bull at Bethel, he was sinning and forfeited the claims of his family to the throne. Hosea views the history with a different and surely with a deeper insight. He is to call his son Jezreel, "for it will not be long, said the Eternal, before I avenge the blood of Jezreel upon the house of Jehu and put an end to the kingdom of Israel. On that day I will break the power of Israel in the valley of Jezreel".[2] On this Mr Elliott Binns comments, "Hosea takes a very different view of the massacre of Ahab's sons from that of the writer of II Kings x. 30. It is important to notice that then, as in all ages, religious opinion was divided over the righteousness of

[1] II Kings x. 30.
[2] Hosea i. 4, 5.

specific events".[1] It is indeed important to remember the difficulty of judging specific events and the likelihood that religious men will differ in their judgments. But it is even more important to notice that the judgment of Hosea is more fundamentally moral than that of the writer of the book of Kings. The clarifying of the prophetic interpretation of history is marked by a growing concern for the fundamental moralities, the condemnation of oppression and cruelty, of injustice and untruthfulness, and the confidence that history will in the long run enforce that condemnation. The remarkable passage from F. W. Robertson's sermon on the Sunday opening of the Crystal Palace in 1851, which has deservedly found a place in *The Oxford Book of English Prose*, illustrates the contrast between a limited Pharisaic moral judgment insisting on positive law and the lesser things of the law, and the true prophetic outlook. The latter must not be confused with the former, though religious men constantly err in this regard, nor must it be dismissed as an example of Philistine moralism. "Now when men are rigorous in the enforcement and reverence paid to laws positive, the tendency is to a corresponding indifference to the laws of eternal Right. The written supersedes in their hearts the moral. The mental history of

[1] S.P.C.K. *Commentary*, p. 558.

the ancient Pharisees who observed the sabbath, and tithed mint, anise, and cummin, neglecting justice, mercy, and truth, is the history of a most dangerous, but universal tendency of the human heart. And so, many a man whose heart swells with what he thinks pious horror when he sees the letter delivered or the train run upon the sabbath-day, can pass through the streets at night, undepressed and unshocked by the evidences of the widespreading profligacy which has eaten deep into his country's heart....No, my brethren! let us think clearly and strongly on this matter. It may be that God has a controversy with this people. It may be, as they say, that our Father will chasten us by the sword of the foreigner. But if He does, and if judgments are in store for our country, they will fall—not because the correspondence of the land is carried on upon the sabbath-day: nor because Sunday trains are not arrested by the legislature: nor because a public permission is given to the working-classes for a few hours' recreation on the day of rest:—but because we are selfish men; and because we prefer Pleasure to Duty and Traffic to Honour; and because we love our party more than our Church, and our Church more than our Christianity; and our Christianity more than Truth, and ourselves more than all. These are the things that defile a nation; but the labour and the recreation of the Poor, these are not the things that defile a nation."[1]

Those who hold to the prophetic standpoint and believe in the inexorable working of moral law have often been weighed down by forebodings of disaster and their forebodings have almost as often been fulfilled. At the beginning of his lectures on the French Revolution, Lord Acton devotes two pages to the teaching of Archbishop Fénelon who challenged the despotism of Louis XIV when it was apparently crowned with success, and revealed the inner rottenness of a system which was doomed to end in ignominy. Alike in his condemnation of Louis XIV and in his anticipations of catastrophe, Fénelon was adopting the prophetic interpretation of history and he was justified by the event.

Lord Acton has also recalled Edmund Burke's remarkable prognostication of the evil that must follow for Europe from the partition of Poland. "No wise or honest man", said Edmund Burke, "can approve of that partition or can contemplate it without prognosticating great mischief from it

[1] It has been pointed out to me that even F. W. Robertson's criterion may be misapplied. Disasters may overtake societies that have not failed in the manner suggested. The conquest of Peru was not explained or justified by the moral failure of the Peruvians, and to insist that calamity always implies immorality is to join oneself to Job's friends.

to all countries at some future time."[1] The full consequences of that crime have only been harvested in our generation, but is it possible to regard as mere chance coincidence the fact that the three imperial houses which participated in that cynical transaction have now fallen from power to dishonour? Is there no suggestion here that as men sow, they reap, and that for every act of oppression and injustice a price has to be paid at the last? The recognition of this truth does not commit anyone to commending the assassination of the Romanoffs as the writer of II Kings might have done. The criminals of Ekaterinburg should remember rather what Hosea said about Jezreel.

It is well known that Gladstone foresaw the nemesis that would follow the annexation of Alsace and Lorraine in 1870. William James likewise foretold another war, as soon as he knew the probable terms of the treaty of Frankfort. The whole of Europe has suffered for the attempt to make that particular injustice part of the public law of Europe. And yet for a generation it looked as if Bismarck had succeeded. So deceptive is the short-period view of events and achievements. Our generation at least, having passed through such fires of judgment, should listen to the prophetic voice which, as Loisy says, for ever sounds through

[1] Acton, *History of Freedom*, p. 275.

history, warning men against reliance on force and reminding them that only justice lasts.[1]

We must keep in mind the general character of prophetic insight into the working of moral law, if we are to judge rightly the prophetic sayings attributed to Jesus in the gospels. The sense of crisis which pervades so many sayings of Jesus can hardly be read back into a ministry which, we are asked to assume, had no such plea for decision. I must not suggest that Jesus spoke and thought of a crisis in the life of the Jewish nation, as we think and speak of a crisis in civilisation. Jesus brought a word of God to His people and asked them to recognise and obey it. He demands surrender and obedience, because positively this is the way of life, not because negatively to refuse obedience is to court death. He bids His people love their enemies, not because in this way they will avoid conflict with Rome but because in this way and only in this way will they become children of their Father in heaven. Yet Jesus is not unaware that the rejection of His message will end not only in individual loss but in national disaster.

In some quarters it is customary to treat all the anticipations of the downfall of Jerusalem as prophecies after the event, and it is difficult to resist the conclusion that the passage in Luke xix. 43, 44,

[1] Cf. *La Morale Humaine*, pp. 216, 217.

has been coloured by the experience of the actual siege of the city. But the suggestion that all the forebodings recorded in the gospels must be treated as afterthoughts should be received with caution. Such a saying as that recorded in Mark xiii. 2, "Seest thou these great buildings? There shall not be left one stone upon another that shall not be thrown down", is a genuine prophetic utterance of Jesus Himself.[1] When I say 'prophetic', I do not mean clairvoyant, but an anticipation based on moral insight.

The threat to this generation (Luke xi. 49–51), the lament over Jerusalem (Matthew xxiii. 37–39), the warning to the daughters of Jerusalem uttered by Jesus on the way to the Cross (Luke xxiii. 28–31), do not really warrant the scepticism with which they are often regarded. There is nothing inherently improbable in the supposition that Jesus Himself applied to the people of His day words which may belong to some form of Wisdom-literature. It is noteworthy that the sayings addressed to the daughters of Jerusalem contain an echo from Hosea.[2] So does the passage in Luke xxi. 22, where reference is made to "days of vengeance or vindication".[3] This phrase also comes from Hosea.

---

[1] See Note D at the end of the chapter.
[2] Cf. Hosea x. 8: "They shall say to the mountains, Cover us: and to the hills, Fall on us".
[3] Cf. Hosea ix. 7: "The days of visitation are come, the days of recompence are come".

We know that Jesus elsewhere appeals to the great passage in Hosea, "I will have mercy and not sacrifice". It would seem as if He found in this prophet, who had with a breaking heart to foretell the overthrow of the kingdom of Israel, a predecessor whose work illuminated his own. Jesus anticipates the downfall of the Jewish State, just as Hosea anticipated the downfall of the Northern kingdom, and He foretells it with Hosea's assurance and compassion.[1]

Saying after saying in the gospels can best be understood if we recognise the fulfilment of the prophetic outlook in Jesus. "Jesus is the stone, rejected of the builders and yet the headstone of the corner. Every one that falls on this stone is broken in pieces." This is the sternest note of warning. "If thou hadst known in this thy day the things concerning thy peace—but now are they hid from thine eyes." This is the tenderest lament.

[1] Kautsky sees in the reference to 'days of vengeance' the expression of a class-hatred more intense than that which prompted the September massacres in the French Revolution. He is assuming that the passage is not prophecy, but a gloating comment on something that has already taken place. But this is a complete misunderstanding. Neither in Hosea from which the phrase comes, nor in the use Jesus makes of it, is there any trace of class-hatred. Hosea at least was no blind proletarian, since he denounced the murders of royalty in Jezreel. Class-hatred is not present, and the sayings may be simply prophetic, contrary to Kautsky's assumption. It was prophetic in the case of Hosea, and there is no reason to question its prophetic character as it stands in the gospels.

Both sayings imply that disaster awaits those who reject Jesus—not those who cannot accept an orthodox creed concerning Him, but those who reject His standards and the truth about God on which those standards rest. "To labour for a perfect redemption from the spirit of oppression is the chief business of the whole family of Christ on earth." That spirit of oppression will continue to bring disaster on mankind until we repent and resolve to have done with it. History is not simply a sad pæan of woe: it is rather a reiterated call to repentance. With no uncertain voice history repeats the appeal of Jesus, re-echoes His inexorable warnings and His wistful invitation.

NOTE D

BULTMANN ON MARK XIII. 2

Bultmann is prepared to allow that the passage in Mark xiii. 2, "Seest thou these great buildings? There shall not be left here one stone upon another that shall not be thrown down", may be a genuine word of the Lord; but this recommendation to mercy is based on the wrong grounds. It is possible, we are told, that Jesus said this, first, because the Jews expected the Messianic age would bring a new and more glorious Temple, and the fulfilment of this hope presupposes the destruction of the old Herodian temple. "The meaning of Mark xiii. 2 need not be anything else than this, and in that case a genuine word of the Lord may lie before us." Secondly, there is a Mandæan

Text which links the destruction of the Temple with cosmic catastrophes, with a destruction of the world which is part of the myth of the primal man. Bultmann is inclined to attribute to this saying of Jesus this mythological origin. Such a discussion seems to me to illustrate the mistake of treating the interpretation of the gospels as a literary rather than a historical problem. Bultmann sees that the first suggestion makes unintelligible the objection taken to this prophecy of Jesus, which in some form or other was brought up in evidence against Him at His trial. It cannot, however, be said that Bultmann's second suggestion makes the objection any more intelligible, even if without evidence we assume, as he does, that some Jewish heretical sect may have associated the destruction of the Temple with the end of the world, as is done in Mark xiii, though not in Mark xiii. 2. But if Jesus foretold the destruction of the Temple as a punishment impending on the Jewish people, and if He spoke in the spirit of Jeremiah, the saying and its effect on Jewish opinion are perfectly intelligible. That Jesus, like one of the ancient prophets, was expressing His faith in the working of moral law in history, is the one possibility which Bultmann never seems to take into account. Yet it is the most likely of all the possibilities we need to consider.

Lecture V

CHRISTIANITY AND PROGRESS

Against thee, thee only, have I sinned, and done that which is evil in thy sight.   PS. LI. 4

For through thy knowledge he that is weak perisheth, the brother for whose sake Christ died.   I COR. VIII. 11.

THE ideas of Progress and Humanity belong apparently to Western culture, and in the West since the Renaissance they have received a secular formulation. Faith in progress is assumed to be something natural and rational, something guaranteed by critical inquiry and by the constitution of human nature. But secular humanism begins to show signs of failure. It lacks intellectual justification and moral power. Can we keep alive our hope for mankind unless we discover some stronger foundation for our faith in progress?

Whatever part rationalists and humanists have played in developing our present-day conceptions of progress, admittedly Christianity paved the way for this development. It was the Christian faith that broke the spell of the Greek idea of a cyclic movement in history, an idea which, taken seriously, deprives the historical process of any real meaning or value. Dr Frederick Temple, in his contribution to *Essays and Reviews*, characterised admirably the contrast between the idea of cyclic change and the idea of progress. He describes how it is possible for the logical understanding to conceive a mechanical universe in which "we should...have a succession of cycles rigidly similar to one another, both in events and in the sequence of them. The universe would eternally repeat the same changes in a fixed order of recurrence, though each cycle might be many millions of years in length". "This supposition transforms the universe into a dead machine. The lives and souls of men become so indifferent, that the annihilation of a whole human race, or of many such races, is absolutely nothing."[1] Against this conception, the spirit of man revolts. In the material world, there may be mere mechanical repetition: in the spiritual world, there must be progress. This rejection of belief in the grand cycle of successive ages was prompted by Christianity.[2]

[1] *Essays and Reviews*, pp. 1, 2.
[2] There is an instance of a curious reversion to the cyclic idea in a well-known Christmas hymn, 'It came upon the midnight clear'. There the writer says:

"For lo! the days are hastening on,
  By prophet-bards foretold,
When with the ever-circling years
  Comes round the age of gold".

This is to accept a Messianic interpretation of Virgil's Fourth Eclogue. It is dubiously Christian.

Bury in his classic on 'The Idea of Progress' has emphasised the importance of this feature of Christianity. Under the influence of Christianity, "the history of the earth was recognised as a unique phenomenon in time: it would never occur again or anything resembling it. More important than all is the fact that Christian theology constructed a synthesis which represents the past as leading up to a definite and desirable goal in the future".[1] This belief in a good time coming, rationalists and humanists subsequently took over, dissociating it from any dependence on providence and any other-worldly reference. The assumption that the idea of progress thereby becomes more rational and satisfying will be examined in the last lecture, but that the germ of the concept was derived from Christianity is not disputed.

The idea of humanity was shaped partly by Alexander's conquests and by the Stoic philosophy. The discovery that the world was a globe— a discovery made or confirmed by the members of Alexander's general staff as they penetrated farther south and east in the invasion of India[2]— suggested dreams of mankind united in a world-wide empire. The Stoic grasped the idea of a common humanity. Christianity regarded the human

[1] *Idea of Progress*, p. 22.
[2] I owe this observation to Dr Ruth von Schulze-Gaevernitz.

race as one, and both deepened and strengthened the idea of humanity by associating it with the moral universalism of the prophets and the appeal of the gospel. Once again Bury, in his lectures on *The Ancient Greek Historians*, stresses the contribution of Christianity to the thought of the solidarity of mankind. "Christianity served to emphasize and intensify the idea of the unity of mankind which had already been preached by the Stoics.... With the Christians the idea acquired a real and intense meaning inasmuch as they believed all the inhabitants of the earth to have a common vital interest, though they might not know it, in the Christian dispensation. In so far as it accustomed men to realise the conception of a solidarity among all the races of humanity, the Christian interpretation assisted in the transition from the ancient to the modern conception of universal history."[1] Thus the ideas of progress and of humanity have been intimately connected with Christianity, and the connection can neither be ignored with justice nor severed without loss.

The Christian interpretation of history as embodied in traditional theology possessed defects which are now obvious and imposed limitations on historical research which were indefensible. Bury justly complains that the price paid for the

[1] *The Ancient Greek Historians*, p. 239.

transition from the ancient to the modern conception of universal history under the ægis of
Christianity was the suspension of free enquiry for
centuries. We may add that the time-perspective
of the drama of redemption which was the real
meaning of history to the Christian has been found
to be hopelessly astray. The history of man on
earth extends backwards through ages uncon-
templated in the Biblical myths of human origins.
The prospects of the continuance of human society
on earth lengthen out beyond the expectations of
those Christian thinkers who were least eschato-
logical and millenarian in their outlook. The time-
perspective of the well-known hymn, "Far down
the ages now, her journey well-nigh done", inevitably evokes a smile from the modern Christian who must learn to think of his religion as still
very young, and who must believe as never before
that with the Almighty a thousand years are but
as one day. No longer can we think of the Fall
as an historic event of a few thousand years ago,
and of the consummation of history and the final
judgment as likely to take place within a measurable period of time. Our whole conception of the
drama of redemption requires to be refashioned.
Moreover, redemption was conceived too narrowly and too exclusively as deliverance from
this present evil world. The idea of the redemption

of society—an idea which has its own difficulties and ambiguities—admittedly played too small a part in the Christian interpretation of history in ancient and mediæval times. To many minds it will seem that the motif of redemption needs to be re-expressed in terms of the education of humanity. The germ of such a philosophy of history might be found in St Paul's saying, "the law was our schoolmaster or slave attendant to bring us to Christ", but the interpretation so suggested has not yet been worked out in a satisfactory and impressive form.

It was natural then that men should break away from the Christian conception of development in history, and should find the scheme of which the leading features were the Fall, Redemption, and the Last Judgment, inadequate and even irrelevant for the guidance of their activities here and now. So in the modern world, faith in progress and a concern to promote progress have tended to replace belief in salvation and a concern to secure men's salvation. Men came to believe that mankind is slowly advancing in a definite and desirable direction, and the advance was expected to continue indefinitely. The idea of progress, Bury observes, implies that "as the issue of the earth's business, a condition of general happiness will be ultimately enjoyed, which will justify the whole process of civilisation: for otherwise the direction would not be desirable".[1] To the humanists of the Renaissance and after, it was not enough to believe that a process was occurring on earth which would in time produce something like an earthly paradise, and which we might further, and in furthering which, might find our happiness. This process must be assured and inevitable, must depend on man's efforts only, and be guaranteed by man's nature. "The process must be the necessary outcome of the psychical and social nature of man: it must not be at the mercy of any external will: otherwise there would be no guarantee of its continuance and its issue and the idea of Progress would lapse into the idea of Providence."[2]

This implication may be regarded as the special contribution of rationalism to the idea of progress. Rationalism fostered the idea of progress as automatic, necessary and inevitable, the idea which seems so remote from reality in our post-war world. It was rationalism which set out to find some law embodying physical or psychical necessity and guaranteeing progress. Bury sympathetically chronicled the stages of the quest and faithfully reported its final failure. No such law has been discovered, and no such law ever will be dis-

[1] *Idea of Progress*, p. 5.   [2] *Op. cit.* p. 5.

covered. For, as is clear from Temple's analysis, any idea of necessity, mechanical or quasi-mechanical, is fatal to the idea of progress. If the rationalists had succeeded in discovering the kind of law for which they were looking, the idea of progress must have lapsed back into the idea of cycles. At the best, they would have arrived at a morphology of history, like Spengler's, and a formula for the rise and decay of civilisation would have engulfed their naïve faith in progress.

The attempt to dissociate progress from providence is prompted by the desire of the rationalist to escape from the reality of God. There is no genuine contrast between faith in progress and faith in providence. The alternatives to providence are not progress, but chance and fate or natural necessity. If the rationalist believes in chance, progress becomes quite uncertain. Its continuance and its issue are at the mercy not indeed of an external will but of sheer blind accident. If, however, the rationalist believes in fate or necessity, the continuance of the process is guaranteed, but not the continuance of progress. The very idea of progress is evacuated of meaning, for progress is the realisation of some good and desirable end, and the realm of necessity or fate is not the realm of ends.

It is characteristic of rationalism to trust nature and man blindly, and to regard God as capricious.

Progress, so the argument runs, is certain if it depends on man, doubtful if it depends on the external capricious will of God. The spell of rationalism is broken for anyone who realises that this confidence in man and nature is as foolish and irrational as this distrust of God. Recent history and Freudian psychology alike remind us that if progress depends on the psychical and social nature of man, its continuance and its issue are highly problematic. Ultimately, the hope of progress is linked with trust in providence. And, in any case, the modern no longer believes in the necessity of progress, but only in its possibility. If progress is possible for us, it is ethically conditioned. The realisation of the possibilities open to us depends on our recognition of and obedience to the demands of the moral order.

If we ask what we mean by progress, the notion that it could be the necessary outcome of some immutable natural process or processes will be seen to be irrelevant and self-contradictory. Our modern belief in progress rests mainly on the advance of knowledge. The development of our understanding and control of the external physical world is actual, undeniable, and cumulative in character. We know more, much more, about the heavens above us than any previous generation has ever known. And we have advanced by building on the work of our predecessors. If modern astronomical theories supersede older theories, the observations of the earliest astronomers are still essential elements in the foundations of our knowledge. In every direction, progress in science, theoretical and applied, is manifest, and calls for constant readjustment in our ways of thinking and in our ways of living. Buckle was not mistaken in regarding the growth of knowledge as the primary factor in the development of civilisation. There is no reason to think that this scientific advance is coming to a halt, and there is no marked sign of any such loss of confidence in reason and in scientific method as initiated the decline of imperial Rome. I say, 'no *marked* sign', because one may well be disturbed by some of the anti-intellectual movements of the present time both in philosophy and in practical politics. But scientists within their own sphere of research do not appear to be losing confidence in their technique, and there is no evidence of a slackening either in the zest of the inquirers or in the success of their inquiries. But we must remember that this advance of science is strictly historical in its nature. It is certainly not automatic or mechanical. No laws which the psychologist and sociologist may discover will ever account for this progress in knowledge or enable you to predict its future course. Still less will any laws which the physicist may discover throw any light on a strictly historical process. The historian alone can describe the actual advance for us, and in the end he must suggest to us, as Bury does, that it is "a disclosure of spiritual reality", "a movement of reason disclosing its nature in terrestrial circumstances".

Can we discern progress in other cultural interests besides the realm of scientific knowledge? Can we affirm progress in art and literature, in religion and morality, in law and politics? In most of these realms, interrelated and yet distinct, progress differs somewhat in character from the advance in scientific knowledge. In the latter realm, the work of pioneers is more fully absorbed into the findings of the present than can ever be the case in art and literature. The achievements of great artists remain as concrete wholes and as abiding sources of inspiration. The essence of such achievements is not absorbed into later artistic productions which do not necessarily surpass and never supersede the works of earlier artists. Copernicus supersedes the Ptolemaic astronomy, and if Einstein be right, his theories absorb whatever was essentially true in Newton and reaffirm it in a better form. But modern music, though it adds new values, neither supersedes nor absorbs nor surpasses the achievements of Bach and

Beethoven. In this realm we are only better than our fathers because we have more achievements to treasure, not because the most recent achievements are superior to those that came earlier in history, or render such earlier creations superfluous. Shaw may be a greater dramatist than Shakespeare, but his superiority will not be due merely to the fact that Shaw emerges later than Shakespeare in the stream of time. Those of us who hesitate to follow Mr Shaw's lead on this issue can at least recognise that the body of dramatic literature is enriched, now that it embraces Shaw as well as Shakespeare. Progress in literature will not mean that later works are necessarily better than earlier ones, but that our store of memorable achievements is perpetually enlarging.

The distinction I am trying to draw here may illuminate a question which perplexes many minds. If our idea of progress be determined by the concept of biological evolution or by the nature of the advance in scientific knowledge, we shall be constantly offended at any suggestion of finality in the claims made for Jesus. Jesus, we shall say, is to be superseded, like Ptolemæus or Newton, and Christianity must be absorbed in some more spiritual religion, presumed to be higher because later. But if the realm of moral and religious insight be parallel rather to the realm of art than to that of science, then we can see that what we may reverently call the achievement or creative act of Jesus may be, nay, will be, unique and irreplaceable, a perpetual and indispensable source of inspiration. Jesus is no more likely to be surpassed or superseded than Bach or Beethoven, and His finality is more significant than theirs, just in so far as truth in religion and morality are more important than the emotive and interpretative power of music. It is possible to see that the progress of mankind in religion and in morals may be a reality, while Jesus remains in some sense final. Indeed, such progress may depend on recognising that He is final, that His trust in God is justified, and His standards of human relations ultimate. In this way, we might understand the amazing saying in the Fourth Gospel, "Greater things than these shall ye do, because I go to the Father".

We must, I think, insist that progress is essentially the enrichment of the cultural traditions of mankind and the development of forms of social organisation and educational methods which will enable an increasing proportion of mankind freely to appropriate and enjoy their growing inheritance. There may be development of mental capacity, but this is of subordinate interest compared with the extension of actual knowledge. Intellectual progress should be interpreted not in terms of capacity but of attainment. If old Dr South was mistaken when he described Aristotle as the veritable rubbish of an Adam, it would be equally wrong to describe the Greek philosopher as the rubbish of an Einstein. There is no reason to suppose that the ancients would have found greater difficulties in intelligence tests than we do. No doubt, as Mr Gerald Heard says, "the real advance insistent but elaborate and concealed, is in man's spirit and can only be disclosed through the evolution of his standards",[1] but the advance in man's spirit is due to his being in truer contact with a wider environment. It is the content of consciousness rather than its form, which really develops. And Mr Gerald Heard seems to me to have overstressed the *form* of consciousness. His theory is that man's consciousness was once pre-individual, a group-consciousness in short, and that it is by now mainly individual, men having become separated as a result of clarifying their ideas and instituting private property. In the modern world, a super-individual type or form of consciousness is evolving. But there is throughout the process described, no change in the fundamental form of consciousness; and if there be any change in the form of consciousness, such change

[1] Gerald Heard, *The Ascent of Humanity*, p. 9.

would not constitute the essence of progress. Consciousness is necessarily individual from start to finish. In reality evolution takes place in men's standards, but these standards are moral and cultural rather than psychological. Throughout, Mr Heard tends to confuse individuality in the sense of self-awareness with individualism in the sense of morally reprehensible self-assertion or psychologically morbid introversion.[1]

Up to a point, however, I am prepared to follow Mr Gerald Heard in the distinction he draws between humanism and humanitarianism, and in the importance he attaches to both as the essential elements in an advanced and progressive civilisation. By humanism he means the intellectual solidarity of mankind, maintained most surely by the great scientific tradition which we owe to the Greeks. Every one is a humanist who accepts the discipline of science and who opens his mind to what are now frequently called 'public' truths. That humanism in this sense is becoming and must become an integral part of a world-civilisation, is beyond dispute. By humanitarianism, Mr Heard understands emotional solidarity and sensibility. To be one with our fellows in the acceptance of common standards of truth is a great thing, but it does not of itself create the sense of kinship which

[1] See Note E at the end of the chapter.

characterises the man of humanitarian sentiment. A scientific humanist is not necessarily a humanitarian, and indeed thinkers like Bertrand Russell and Aldous Huxley forecast the development of a scientific society which will ruthlessly discard anything in the nature of humanitarianism. Mr Heard sees that both humanism and humanitarianism are essential to progress, though he recognises that they do not automatically harmonise and reinforce one another.

To coordinate these two elements, faith in reason and belief in the solidarity of mankind, we must, in my judgment, be Christians. The Christian religion alone can check our constant tendency to divorce heart and head, because it is vitally concerned to maintain respect for truth and respect for personality. The positive contribution of Christianity to intellectual freedom and to the advance of knowledge is none the less actual because it is the fashion to ignore it. I may be allowed to remind you that the great advance in methods of historical enquiry took place in the field of church history, and was largely the work of men of positive faith. But the connection of Christianity with humanitarianism is even more intimate. It is at this point that Mr Gerald Heard's treatment of his theme seems to me most disappointing and inadequate. He finds the basis of humanitarianism in an intuitive feeling for others, and this feeling has developed through the influence of pioneers like Akhnaton, through the artistic sensibilities of the Greeks, through the teaching of Socrates and his disciples, and through the gracious personality of the Buddha. Nowhere in *The Ascent of Humanity* does Mr Heard mention Jesus, yet the humanitarian sentiment in the West undeniably owes more to Him than to any other influence. Loisy is proclaiming an objective historic truth when he says that the feeling for humanity, which he regards as the best thing in our Western civilisation, has come to us from the gospel.[1]

Regard it how we will, as a matter of actual history Christianity, in Bury's phrase, emphasised and intensified the idea of the unity of mankind. The Christian believed himself and all his fellows to be the objects of God's mercy. The dignity and worth of man is bound up with the fact that God has visited and redeemed His people. It is possible to entertain an emotional solidarity on another basis, but no other basis for humanitarianism has the same intensity and reality.

Mr Gerald Heard ignores Jesus, because he believes in a purely secular form of humanitarianism. Any form of humanitarianism which derives its valuation of men from the sense of something

[1] Cf. *La Morale Humaine*, p. 251 f.

beyond is to him anathema. He has already dismissed in advance the mystic and the monk as examples of lower individuality diverted by superstition from its natural secular development and so asserting its claims in another world. Such an estimate of mysticism and monasticism is in the strict sense unhistorical. It is the judgment of one who has not really asked himself, what has been the actual character and influence in history of mysticism and monasticism? Anyone who does ask the question seriously will know that such movements cannot be summarised and dismissed in a formula.

It is a strange perversity of outlook to imagine that super-personality is only now emerging in history for the first time. If the emergence of super-personality means anything, it means the emergence of that type of character which subordinates one's self to love of truth and love of one's fellows. But such characters have been present all through history and most notably within the sphere of influence of the Christian tradition. There is no reason to suppose that we are richer in super-personalities or upper-individualities to-day than we were in the Middle Ages. Just as the great thinkers in the Middle Ages exhibit in their own manner and degree the intellectual solidarity of mankind, and just as we did not have to wait for the Renaissance to recover the habit of honest thinking, so the great mystics, monks and friars and heretics, are not so many examples of lower individuality, but give form to that deeper feeling for humanity to which we must be loyal to-day.

If we turn back to the saints of the dark ages, we shall find in the records not the safety-valve of a turbulent stream of psychic energy seeking expression in individuality, but the heroic maintenance of the humanitarian sentiment. We must be very blind if behind the naïve supernaturalism and often repulsive asceticism of those legends of the saints, we cannot see the spiritual counterweight to the grossness and violence of the times in which these men lived. Some sentences from Samuel Dill, *Roman Society in Gaul in the Merovingian Age*, will suffice to illustrate the argument. "The reader, indeed, will often be shocked and disgusted by austerities and self-inflicted torture which seem to violate all instincts of self-respect. On the other hand, he will meet with the tenderest, most delicate sympathy, rare in such an age, for all the misery inflicted by high-handed oppression, for the cruelties of war, for poverty or loathsome disease. Moral force is asserting itself fearlessly and, at times, triumphantly against overbearing physical force, whether of the crowd or of the great. Pity, gentleness, and tenderness of heart, compassion for all weak things, are revealing their strange power against brutal arrogance and selfishness."[1] And again, Dill writes: "In the effort of the human spirit to find avenues to the remote Supreme and Infinite, through many ages in heathendom and Christendom, the pious imagination has sought many mediators in a celestial hierarchy, linking the human and the Divine; and, if the adoration of saints had its lower side, it also consecrated high and rare examples of spiritual refinement, detachment, self-abnegation and also of boundless charity and pity for the victims of oppression, desire, and want. If it gave its heroes superhuman rank and powers, it also held up before a gross age an ideal of those qualities which have moulded modern civilisation. Severe purity, charity to the poor and afflicted, at the cost of immense self-sacrifice, were an influence and a pattern which the world then needed, and the need for which has not ceased".[2]

The saints of the dark ages and their successors in mediæval times are a bugbear to modern humanists, because they were uncompromisingly otherworldly and confessed that they were strangers and pilgrims in search of a better country. If they contributed to progress, they did so without believing in it. For them the times were waxing evil, and they expected the arrival of Antichrist

---

[1] *Op. cit.* p. 409.　　[2] P. 424.

rather than the attainment of a desirable goal on earth. They were very much on the defensive, clinging to the remnants of a dying culture rather than consciously building up a new order, and thankful for a confident hope in another life since the present world was so obviously in desperate plight. And yet their faith kept the note of romance and adventure alive, as Samuel Dill points out. To these men life was full of strange and oft-times glorious possibilities. It is more of a paradox to discover that through these men with all their otherworldliness, the sense of kinship with nature and the love of nature revived. A noteworthy feature recurrent in the legends of the saints is the friendly relations established between the saint and some wild animal. This one befriends a wild boar, that a stag, and that other a wild bull. This feature of Merovingian legends recalls Jerome and his lion and points on to St Francis. Among the monks was developed not only the will to reclaim but the leisure to appreciate the countryside. In St Francis this sense of kinship with nature reaches its high-water mark. It is a remarkable characteristic of men whose crime in modern eyes is that they denied the earth for their fatherland. Maybe, after all, to enjoy nature we must believe in the supernatural.

The saints won their way to the affections of the

common folk because their attitude was the safe-guard of the dignity and worth of the common people. And in this connection we must not think only of the large-hearted charity which such men practised, or of dramatic actions like that of St Francis in embracing a leper. The recognition of the actual rather than the potential worth of the obscure and the humble is even more important. The stories told of Egyptian monks and hermits may be more impressive in this regard. There is the story of St Anthony discovering in a simple working carpenter in Alexandria a more holy man than himself. Hugh Latimer related it in the following terms:

"We read a pretty story of St Anthony, who, being in the wilderness, led there a very hard and strait life, insomuch that none at that time did the like; to whom came a voice from heaven saying, 'Anthony, thou art not so perfect as a cobbler that dwelleth at Alexandria'. Anthony, hearing this, rose up forthwith and took his staff and went till he came to Alexandria, where he found the cobbler. The cobbler was astonished to see so reverend a father come to his house. Then Anthony said to him, 'Come and tell me thy whole conversation, and how thou spendest thy time'. 'Sir,' said the cobbler, 'as for me, good works have I none, for my life is but simple and slender. I am but a poor cobbler: in the morning when I rise, I pray for the city wherein I dwell, specially for all such neighbours and poor friends as I have; after, I set me at my labour, where I spend the whole day in getting my living, and I keep me from falsehood, for I hate nothing so much as deceitfulness; wherefore, when I make to any man a promise, I keep it and perform it truly: and so I spend my time poorly with my wife and children, whom I teach and instruct, so far as my wit will serve me, to fear and dread God. And this is the sum of my simple life.'

"In this story you see how God loveth those that follow their vocation and live uprightly, without any falsehood in their dealing. This Anthony was a great, holy man, yet the cobbler was as much concerned before God as he."

A similar story is told of an Egyptian monk who was directed to visit a certain shepherd and learn of him. The shepherd expounded his simple manner of life. "Behold these thirty years, more or less, I have never tasted anything else than these herbs which I have eaten once a day, and I drink as much water as my food requireth; and the wages which are given to me by the owner of the sheep, I give unto the poor." And we are told, the monk "marvelled how many were the saints in the world who were not known to the children of men ".[1] Our sense of the true dignity of man may depend on such recognition of the unknown soldiers of the spirit of humanity.

The contribution of mediæval Christianity to humanitarianism might be illustrated at much greater length. Has humanitarianism in the modern world other roots and other supports? The revival of humanism with its secularist bias has undoubtedly helped to make men more humane. The spirit of Montaigne, for example, is a spirit of easy and even wise tolerance. Humanism and rationalism have restrained the inhumanities of theologians and put a curb on cruelties based on superstition. On the other hand, the renascence of Greek humanism has also helped to undermine the sense of the sacredness of personality, and has sometimes favoured the cynicism and brutalities of so-called realists in politics and in industry. Machiavelli was an emancipated renascence humanist. Actually, the spirit of the classics, Greek and Roman, will not suffice to maintain humanitarianism in the modern world. The development of a deeper feeling for humanity since the Reformation has in fact been largely dependent on Christian influences.

According to Mr Gerald Heard, the emotional solidarity and sensibility appropriate to the modern

[1] *Paradise of the Fathers*, Part III, § 104 (Vol. II, pp. 23, 24, ed. Budge).

super-personality appear first among the Quakers in an effective form. He attributes the philanthropy of the early Friends to their discerning that the individual cannot be saved without the whole. It is certainly true that George Fox is distinguished from the Ranters by his realisation of the social implications of his faith in the Inward Light. With the Ranters, this claim to individual guidance and inspiration issued in spiritual anarchy, each man becoming a law unto himself. Fox saw that the truth of God's guidance of individuals did not make men independent of one another but rather determined the character of the relations which should subsist between men. To him, the recognition of something of God in our fellows is the basis of friendship, and so the principle on which may be built and maintained a Christian order of society. But all the teaching and organising work of Fox depended not on a sociological doctrine to the effect that the individual cannot be saved without society, nor yet on a community sense which swamped his individual consciousness out of existence, but on the contrary it depended on an intense inward experience of God in Christ, in which he felt himself peculiarly isolated and alone, and through which he learned to appreciate more fully and respect more deeply the mystery of each man's inner life. There is no deeper feeling for humanity which does not spring from an intenser individuality, a deeper sense of the mystery and worth of personality. Fox stands almost exactly where the early Christians stood. They believed that all men were vitally concerned in the Christian dispensation. So did Fox. Because every child of man has his day of divine visitation, we may despise no man and must hope for all. The humanitarianism of the Friends rests on their religious experience and convictions, on their awareness of God's guidance, on their consciousness of the presence of the living Christ.

In some ways John Bunyan is in strong contrast to George Fox, yet his *Pilgrim's Progress* with its intense individualism is a classical contribution to emotional solidarity and sensibility. That picture of the life of the individual as a lonely spiritual pilgrimage is a tremendous assertion of the dignity of human nature. The book enabled thousands of humble folk to understand their true selves. It enabled them to realise something of the romance of their inner life. That self-analysis and reflection on one's self have often taken on morbid forms cannot be denied. There are morbid traits in *Grace Abounding*, and material for the abnormal psychologist in *The Journal of George Fox*. But the remarkable fact apparent in these two examples, and by no means confined to them, is the power of the

Christian faith to counteract the poison of a morbid scrupulosity and to heal the diseases of divided personalities. Both Bunyan and Fox were really saved by faith. And Christianity makes it possible for men to be sincere and open with themselves. Hence we have in Augustine a new type of man. The *Confessions* become a classic in psychology, and not primarily in morbid psychology, but in psychology in the only true sense of the word. The *Confessions* are a contribution to our knowledge of the soul of man. Now this deepening of the inner life of the individual and of the individual's understanding of the mystery of his selfhood is absolutely essential to any vital and enduring humanitarianism. An emotional solidarity devoid of the sense of personal worth is socially valueless. That the individual cannot be saved without society is an important truth. That society cannot be saved without deepening the inner life of the individual is still more important. No humanitarianism is worthy of the name that does not foster self-respect. And it follows that the *Pilgrim's Progress* is a humanitarian classic.

If we turn to the eighteenth century, there is no need to belittle the contribution to humanitarian sentiment made by the Deists and the French rationalists of the Enlightenment. Voltaire, Diderot, Condorcet and many others will recur to the mind among those who have advanced the cause of humanity. Yet here too Rousseau and the Romanticists, poets and novelists, have surely done more than the rationalists to foster respect for ordinary human nature. Wordsworth's *Leech-gatherer* is probably a more vital factor in promoting emotional solidarity and sensibility than the philosophy of Jeremy Bentham, which treats men as units rather than persons.[1] And after all, Methodism and the Evangelical Revival did more even than Romanticists and rationalists combined. The greatest single triumph of humanitarianism in the first half of the nineteenth century was the abolition of slavery. In the main, though not exclusively, it was the work of men whose inspiration was distinctly Christian.

The centenary of the freeing of slaves in the British Empire, and the centenary of the birth of the Oxford Movement have both claimed our attention this year.[2] At first sight there is little or no connection between the two movements, and yet in its actual development, if not in its inception, the Oxford Movement has made a noteworthy contribution to the humanitarian spirit. It is not an accident that a movement which in its origin

[1] Compare a penetrating criticism of Leonard Woolf, "After the Deluge", by Helen Wodehouse, in the *Hibbert Journal*, July 1932, pp. 700–704. Whitehead (*Adventures of Ideas*, p. 48) justly observes that Bentham and Comte "have gained nothing in the way of certainty by dropping Plato and Religion".

[2] 1933.

was politically and socially conservative in temper, discovered affinities with socialism and responded to the teachings of F. D. Maurice and the Christian Socialists more readily than the men of the Evangelical tradition. F. D. Maurice's impressive though difficult conception of humanity as already in Christ, belonging to Christ and influenced by Christ's spirit, was reinterpreted in the Catholic doctrine of the church as the body of Christ and in the High Churchman's emphasis on the sacramental principle. Here was a community sense which recognised the dependence and demanded the loyalty of the individual, and this was a valid insight, even if at times loyalty and dependence were mistakenly interpreted in terms of blind submission to traditional standards and authorities. In the sacramental principle, which stresses the spiritual significance and influence of outward things, was found a fresh incentive to work for decent, healthy, and beautiful surroundings for all. In the sacraments themselves was discovered an assertion of spiritual equality and of Christian fellowship which called for more adequate social expression. If in some of its manifestations the Catholic Revival has not always been worthy of its name, tempting men as Newman himself was tempted to overvalue tradition and to distrust the contemporary inspiration of the Holy Ghost, encouraging some to lose their sense of proportion over liturgical detail, and leading others to set arbitrary limits to the Christian fellowship, yet in some of its essentials it has fostered the growth of the humanitarian sentiment. It has challenged social degradation and reminded us that we are members one of another.

If it were possible to write the history of humanitarianism we should find that it is not distinctively modern. It has been a slow growth for which in the days of Imperial Rome and in the dark and middle ages Christianity was primarily responsible. This sentiment did not come into existence with the Reformation or owe its modern development primarily to the recovery of the Greek tradition. If in the modern world the influence of Christianity crosses with the influence of Greek humanism, just as it intermingled with the influence of Stoicism in the world of the early Roman Empire, it does not on that account become one whit less real or less important. Humanitarianism in its modern form is as closely associated with Christianity as it ever was. As Lord Acton said of the four hundred years of modern history, "even this narrow and disedifying section of history will aid you to see that the action of Christ who is risen on mankind whom he redeemed fails not, but increases".[1]

[1] *Lectures on Modern History*, p. 12.

Humanitarianism is of course possible on the basis of naturalism, but it is likely to prove disappointing. Emotional solidarity of itself is not enough. The value of such experience depends on the sincerity and depth of the emotions, and on the reality and character of the objects which evoke the emotional response. Our feeling for the oneness of humanity will be little worth if our valuation of the individual is steadily declining. Mr J. W. N. Sullivan has a paragraph in his autobiographical novel, *But for the Grace of God*, which describes, in my judgment truly, the lowered quality apparent in modern secular humanitarianism.

"I suggest that the standards generally accepted at the present day are quite probably insufficient and misleading. The novelists from whom we have derived them have not been sufficiently penetrating. The present-day cynical attitude towards 'greatness' is an indication that this may be true. The kind of understanding of human nature that we have accepted has very largely freed us from self-contempt by showing us how natural and universal our 'lapses' are, but it has also made us very sceptical of heroic achievement. Sins have been turned into more or less amiable weaknesses, but also sanctity and heroism have become myths. The human being as a whole has been made smaller.

The novelists have convinced us that the average human being is compounded out of a few paltry vices and a fairly large slab of good nature. Christ who called us sons of God and Swift who called us little odious vermin, are both making a quite unnecessary fuss about almost nothing."[1]

"The human being as a whole has been made smaller." Man is bound to shrivel into insignificance, if he surrenders his spiritual birthright. The sinner who realises that he has to do with God and not simply with society, who can say, "Against thee, thee only, have I sinned"—the scientist who recognises that in making discoveries he is not simply enunciating 'public' truths, but 'trafficking with eternities'—the simple believer who knows that men do not live by bread alone but by the word of God—the poet who knows that in mystery the soul abides—these keep alive the true spirit of man. Boutroux has finely said of the great men in Comte's calendar, "They are in Comte's calendar because they did not believe in Comte's creed".[2] The men who have done most to raise humanity have believed in something beyond humanity.

[1] *Op. cit.* pp. 117–18.
[2] "La foi dans la réalité supérieure d'un objet idéal, irréductible à tout le donné, a produit les héros qu'honore à bon droit Aug. Comte: ils sont les saints de son calendrier, parce qu'ils n'ont pas cru à son religion", *Science et Religion*, p. 77.

The elusive idea of equality is also likely to degrade humanity. The solidarity of mankind will not be furthered by what Mr Sullivan calls our cynical present-day attitude towards greatness. He has elaborated this in another paragraph.

"There are people, I know, who think the 'great man' is a sort of myth. They will admit a quantitative difference, as it were, between men, but not a qualitative difference. The great man is merely a larger edition of the small man. I think this is true of some men whom we would have to call great, but I do not think that it is generally true. There are artists who express for us what we already know: there are other artists who present to us our familiar world in an entirely new light, and who even reveal to us an entirely new world. The sensibilities of such artists may be essentially similar to our own, but the synthesis of the experience they have effected is something radically new. The work of such men is, it seems to me, prophetic of the future development of the human consciousness. . . . The great men of my youth were truly great men and *greater than I knew*." [1]

The contrast between J. W. N. Sullivan and Lytton Strachey immediately suggests itself. To breathe a word in dispraise of the work of Lytton Strachey is to invoke the anathemas of the most

---

[1] *But for the Grace of God*, p. 73.

modern of our modern critics. But the issue is clear enough. I do not doubt that Lytton Strachey was as charming and delightful, as happy and contented as his friends say he was. I humbly take my place in the circle of his admirers and enjoy almost to the full his often delicate irony, his often pungent wit, and his occasional impish irreverence. I can appreciate his literary genius and his intellectual alertness as I appreciate Lucian or Montaigne or Anatole France, and I realise how much his qualities as a thinker and writer depend on the sceptical humanism which constituted his outlook. I value highly the contribution he has made to the art of biography. But when all is said in praise of Lytton Strachey, as essays in interpretation and portraiture the studies of 'Eminent Victorians' were a failure. And they failed because Lytton Strachey was a sceptical humanist, because what meant everything to the subjects of his portraits meant nothing to the artist. In consequence his studies in iconoclasm were entertaining, unconventional, stimulating, but ungenerous and untrue, and necessarily untrue because inevitably ungenerous. Our feeling for humanity will grow thin and sour, if we lose our capacity for recognising and reverencing true greatness in our fellows. Whatever possibilities of progress lie open to mankind, their realisation depends on the depth and sincerity of the humanitarian sentiment. We shall not maintain our sense of human dignity and worth by flattering ourselves or by ignoring the limitations of ordinary human nature. Man's power to rise depends on his power to recognise the things that are excellent. We shall not then elevate mankind if we belittle or ignore Jesus. Progress depends more intimately than we often remember on recognising His intrinsic greatness. Dr Schweitzer described the quest for the historic Jesus as a failure, implying, it would seem, that Jesus was so much involved in the time and circumstances of the first century that He could never be anything but a stranger to the twentieth. This is not, however, the true significance of the felt inadequacy of the liberal portrait of Jesus. The failure of the quest is really the discovery that Jesus is greater than we know. We are faced once more with the paradox that the mystery of His person and character baffles the wisest and most learned, and yet He is "dear intimate of little folk". Our hopes for mankind rest on the faith that men are Christ's brethren and that for them He died. The recognition of the essential greatness of Jesus and of the consequent marvel of His laying down His life for every man is the surest basis for our combined faith in the worth of the individual and the solidarity of mankind.

NOTE E

MR GERALD HEARD'S CONCEPTION OF
PSYCHIC ENERGY

Mr Gerald Heard believes in a stream of psychic energy, which by some necessity of its nature must express itself in a succession of types of individuality, and is now of necessity passing beyond individuality. The influence of the lower aggressive types of individuality can be traced through the succession of priest-kings and witch-doctors who are followed by warrior-heroes, mystics or monks. Monasticism canalised and sidetracked individuality, but after the Renaissance it resumed its development as a secular phenomenon and gave us the revolutionary age. We have had three revolutions in Europe, religious, political, and economic, which all follow the same forms of procedure whereby inquiry and criticism culminate in an emotional challenge. There is a false simplification of the issues in the revolutionary's diagnosis of human life. "Get rid of priests and all will be well", says Luther in effect. "Get rid of despots and all will be well", cries Rousseau. "Get rid of capitalists and all will be well", declares Marx. Mass upheaval sweeps away the scapegoats and engenders the inevitable reaction. But there is emerging a higher type of individuality which sees to the end of the revolutionary age. The upper-individuality shows that individuality's climax has been passed, by linking up with the science of the Greeks in Humanism and with the deepening of feeling in Humanitarianism. This super-personality is marked by a new community sense, for progress is spiral, and we recover something like the primitive group-consciousness, on a higher level.

There is much that is suggestive in Mr Gerald Heard's *Ascent of Humanity*, whose argument I have thus crudely outlined. But his concept of the stream of psychic energy is pure myth and the *necessity* of its actual development is assumed without evidence. Moreover, Mr Gerald Heard has accepted too readily M. Lévy-Bruhl's theories of savage mentality together with the sociology of Émile Durkheim. No doubt the savage is more fully aware of his belonging to and depending on his group than the self-made business man is mindful of his relation to his community. But the consciousness of the savage is still his own. It is not pre-individual. And if in the consciousness of the super-personality the community sense is stronger than in the mind of the thrustful individualist, the super-personality is more rather than less of an individual. At no stage was individuality absent and at no stage is it superseded.

Lecture VI

THE RELIGION OF TIME AND THE
RELIGION OF ETERNITY

If in this life only we have hope in Christ, we are of all men most
miserable.   I CORINTHIANS XV. 19

. . .He shewed unto them his hands and his side. Then were the
disciples glad, when they saw the Lord.   JOHN XX. 20

"IT is not for the historian to give a philosophical
explanation of what happens in time and
space. Indeed any history that he writes ought
to be as capable of varied philosophical interpretation as life itself seems to be.''[1] In these sentences,
Mr Butterfield warns the historian against setting
up as the arbiter of philosophical issues, just as he
has previously warned him against playing the rôle
of moral censor. And no doubt in the field of philosophy as in the field of morals, the historian has to
appear not as final arbiter but as expert witness. If,
however, he confines himself to his proper task of
giving evidence, the very nature of history, so disclosed, invites the recognition of the working of a
moral order in the affairs of men and likewise
excludes certain philosophical interpretations as
inadequate to account for the rich world of human

[1] *The Whig Interpretation of History*, p. 71.

experience. History, if it is written with that interest in the concrete, the particular, the personal, which the modern historian knows to be necessary, ought to show that life is not as capable of varied philosophical interpretations as it seems to be. It follows at once from the nature of the historical process that no interpretation of life in terms of mechanistic materialism can be true. As Troeltsch puts it, "History has freed us from mathematical-mechanical concepts of Nature".[1] Such concepts can never give us the whole truth about the real world. No concept of nature drawn from physics or from biology can interpret history. The second law of thermodynamics limits and conditions human history: it does not account for a single event in that history. So William James rightly dismissed the attempt of Henry Adams to explain the historical process by the transformation of physical energy in accordance with laws which the physicist discovers. "The second law", wrote William James, "is wholly irrelevant to 'history' save that it sets a terminus." Nor is it possible to retain the essential position of Henry Adams, in the way Mr Gerald Heard suggests, by substituting for physical energy and physical laws, psychic energy and psychological laws. The generalisations of the psychologist are indeed more relevant to the under-

---

[1] Troeltsch, *Historismus und seine Probleme*, p. 10.

standing of history than the laws of physics. But if Mr Butterfield is right when he says that "the eliciting of general truths or of propositions claiming universal validity is the one kind of consummation which it is beyond the competence of history to achieve", this situation can only arise from the fact that the general truths established in the natural sciences are not competent to explain history. This is a philosophical conclusion to which history as we now are obliged to conceive it inevitably points.

An illustration may serve to enforce the argument. If he had but the time and I had but the brain, Mr Bertrand Russell could explain mathematical physics to me. But it is an illusion to suppose that any advance in mathematical physics would ever explain Mr Bertrand Russell to me. Even psychological categories would not carry me to the end of the journey. I could only hope to reach an understanding of Mr Bertrand Russell, if it were within my reach at all, by adopting the distinctively historical approach.

That Naturalism and Materialism are incompatible with the nature of history is recognised in the very remarkable and comparatively little known address of Bury on "The Place of Modern History in the perspective of Knowledge", an address delivered at St Louis in 1904. Bury's acceptance of

an idealistic position is the more noteworthy because it is really inconsistent with his rationalism.
His work as an historian drives him into a philosophic interpretation which he accepts with re-
luctance. The main passage runs thus: "If human
development can be entirely explained on the
general lines of a system such as Saint Simon's or
Comte's or Spencer's, then I think we must con-
clude that the place of history within the frame
of such a system, is subordinate to sociology and
anthropology. There is no separate or independent
precinct in which she can preside supreme. But
on an idealistic interpretation of knowledge, it is
otherwise. History then assumes a different meaning from that of a higher zoology and is not merely
a continuation of the process of evolution in
nature.... If the philosophy of history is not illusory, history means a disclosure of spiritual
reality in the fullest way in which it is recognisable
to us in these particular conditions. And on the
other hand, the possibility of an interpretation of
history as a movement of reason disclosing its
nature in terrestrial circumstances, seems the only
hypothesis on which the postulate of 'history for
its own sake' can be justified as valid".[1] For
myself, I am convinced that some such philosophy
of history is the only tenable philosophy. The view

[1] *Select Essays*, p. 46.

that any history which the modern historian writes ought to be as capable of varied philosophical interpretation as life itself seems to be, is so far from being true that there is implicit in all modern historical work a philosophical interpretation of a definitely idealistic or spiritual order, and history is not, and ought not to be, susceptible of any other type of interpretation.

If with Bury we recognise that "historical experience is a disclosure of the inner nature of spiritual reality", and that only on the acceptance of this philosophy can we maintain the distinctness and independence of history as a science, it is tempting to follow Croce and identify spiritual reality with the historic process as such. This seems to be the meaning of the cryptic saying, philosophy is history, and Bury would seem to endorse it when he says, the disclosure of spiritual reality is furnished by history and by history alone, so that the philosopher must turn historian in order to be philosopher. Croce appears to hold that there is a universal spirit immanent in but greater than our finite minds, and this universal spirit does not merely express itself in the temporal process but is that process and its content. In this form of idealism, stress falls on the immanence of the spirit, to the exclusion of transcendence. The mistake of religion, in contrast to philosophy, will be its constant positing of a transcendental reality. An idealism of this immanentist order has many attractions. It seems to safeguard history as a science from having to deal with the incursions of an external capricious will—that bugbear of the rationalist. It suggests that the historic process is in the nature of a closed self-explanatory system, the rational principles of which may be discerned. But we cannot help asking whether the type of idealism favoured by Bury and Croce does not involve us in the same sort of mistake with regard to history which philosophers who build primarily on physics or biology have made in the past. Each science isolates a particular aspect of reality and treats it provisionally as a closed system. Since physics and chemistry embrace all our trustworthy knowledge of the vast spaces of the universe, it is tempting to treat this as the most comprehensive disclosure of the nature of reality. The facts of life and consciousness studied in biology and psychology seem so trivial when estimated by any spatial and temporal standards, that it is easy to ignore them, to assume that sooner or later these facts will be subsumed under the headings of physics and chemistry, or at least to dismiss the biologist and psychologist as concerned with very parochial interests. But the historian reminds us first that no science can dispense with brute facts. Every science starts from essentially historical data which cannot be derived from the generalisations used to interpret and describe them. The emergence of distinct sciences and the formation of a hierarchy of sciences, indicates the assumption of additional brute facts as the foundation of each successive isolated system. The methods of the psychologist and biologist may approximate more and more to the methods of the chemist and the physicist, but that does not mean that biology and psychology are being reduced to physics or that the data of life and consciousness are becoming susceptible of interpretation in terms of physical laws. To mistake each isolated aspect of reality for the whole of reality, or to regard each system which we can isolate for scientific purposes as closed, self-contained, and independent, are the most obvious and most recurrent mistakes in philosophy. Every form of naturalism and materialism is but a dreary repetition of these patent illusions, and one of the most grievous defects in higher education is its failure to save those who are exposed to it from confusing the fallacies of naturalism with the findings of science. The study of history should save us from such inadequate philosophies, but if in turn we treat history as ultimate, we may be little better off than the philosophers who take the findings of the physicist as an exhaustive transcript

of reality. We may fairly claim that philosophies
which disregard history must of necessity be false,
but we can hardly claim that the disclosure of the
inner nature of spiritual reality through history is
complete and exhaustive. It is true of course that
our knowledge of Spirit can only come to us in
and through the historical process. But the Spirit
so revealed to us cannot be contained within the
historical process itself. There is something ab-
horrent to the West in the Hindu doctrine of the
universe as Maya or illusion, and yet, as I think
A. G. Hogg points out, there is something splendid
in the Hindu conviction that not simply our universe but a whole series of universes cannot exhaust
Brahma. The heaven of heavens cannot contain
God. Moreover the actual process of history does
not suggest a world of spiritual reality exhaustively
or exclusively expressed in history. The issue here
is bound up with the nature of such dialectic as
may be discerned in history. Is the dialectic
Hegelian or Barthian in character? The value of
the Hegelian dialectic does not depend on its
validity as a key to history. That on every side men
are confronted with pairs of opposite things, that
they tend to treat the oppositions as ultimate and
move from pole to pole only to discover the necessity of a synthesis or reconciliation, is undeniably
true. That the historic process conforms strictly to

such a logical process is, however, not true. It has to be remembered that we ought to speak of processes rather than process, of histories rather than history. We are involved in a series of interacting processes, and the fresh starts apparent in any one of these series may be due to some influence from without. There is no self-contained single process, economic or other, which advances by an immanent dialectic and determines the development of every other human interest. I am quite unable to see with Professor Macmurray that organic development of any kind conforms to a dialectic principle of the Hegelian or the Marxian type.[1] In any case, neither Hegel's dialectic nor any form of organology describes the actual march of history. The course of events reveals rather the dialectic of Barth's theology, God's abrupt No to man's affirmations, or to adopt St Paul's more positive emphasis, God's choice of the weak things of this world to confound the mighty, yea, God's choice of the things that are not to put to shame the things that are. To quote Troeltsch, "Grace and Election are the mystery and the essence of

[1] Professor Macmurray having distinguished the superorganic or personal from the organic relations subsisting among men, ought not to believe with the Marxist that social history is determined by a dialectic development of organic relations. Actual history will be complicated by the existence of these higher relations all the time. See *The Philosophy of Communism*, esp. pp. 17 and 74.

history".[1] Events cannot be fully interpreted in terms of an immanent logic, precisely because the universal spirit is beyond as well as within the process.

Most of our modern religions of time fall short of the intellectual courage and profundity of Croce. Faith in the continued advance of the life-force, or in the progress of humanity constitutes the popular form of this-world religion. But life, progress, humanity, when regarded as the ultimate or highest values, will be found to be irrational and unsatisfying. Life is not really worth while, unless we believe in something more than life. Progress which must come to an end has no abiding value, and never-ending progress in time on this earth, even if we might hope for it, would be stale, flat and unprofitable. Humanity cannot be the ultimate reality, and in spite of Comte and Dr McTaggart is a poor substitute for God.

Bury notes that though the idea of progress has been accepted and formulated in the main by rationalists, who profess to be guided only by the light of reason and scientifically ascertained facts, belief in progress is really an act of faith. "The Progress of Humanity belongs to the same order of ideas as Providence or personal immortality. It is true or it is false, and like them it cannot be

[1] *Historismus*, p. 101.

proved either true or false."[1] Bury, as we have already seen, regards as essential to the idea of progress, the establishment of a condition of general happiness on earth which will justify the whole process of civilisation. Is this a rational, realisable aim? We may hope and expect that particular obstacles to happiness may be removed and overcome, but we may well doubt whether happiness without conflict and danger is possible on earth, and whether a condition of general happiness even if realised and retained for many generations would justify the process of civilisation. The process must be justified to those who paid the price, but on the rationalist hypothesis those who pay the price of progress can never know that their sacrifices have been worth while. And how can posterity enjoy a condition of general happiness, when they realise that those who have made it possible can never share it? It is indeed more than likely that future generations in relation to their predecessors will resemble the unfortunate child in the Punch anecdote whose parents brought it to Hampstead Heath to enjoy itself. Posterity may disappoint the hopes of its progenitors by refusing to enjoy

---

[1] *Memoir*, p. 87. No doubt by proof Bury meant evidence properly sifted. But it is possible to show that even if progress in particular directions be historically actual (and, in spite of Bury, evidence can be produced to substantiate the fact), yet progress in time is ultimately unsatisfying.

or by being unable to enjoy the condition of general happiness painfully provided for it. Even if we could establish a condition of general happiness, the achievement would not of itself be an adequate compensation for the martyrdom of man. Moreover, the achievement itself would accentuate the frustration of death. The more worth while human life can be made on this earth, the greater the sense of loss in leaving it, if this life be all and this earth indeed our fatherland. The fashion of modern humanists in dismissing with contempt the hope of personal immortality often involves an evasion of an ultimate issue. We are to be satisfied, we are told, with the continuance of the race, sink our supposedly selfish claims for our petty individual selves, in the future of humanity or the life-force. But humanity and the life-force itself lie under exactly the same doom as the individual. The future of the race is only an Ersatz-immortality, a spurious and inadequate substitute for the genuine article. For we must face the real implication of the humanist argument. What we individually value, our achievements, our treasured traditions and possessions, so the argument runs, will not be lost because we hand them on to future generations. We should be content to drop into eternal silence, because values will be preserved. But clearly this process will come to an end, and the comfort it brings is illusory. The loss of everything we value is only postponed and not prevented. A reprieve of the sentence of death is no equivalent to the assertion of the conservation of value. If there be no spiritual reality that abides for ever, if in this life only the things we value count and then vanish for ever from the universe, we are miserable. Memory becomes a curse and consciousness a pain, and the tragic sense of life can be avoided only by sinking back to the animal level. Some humanists actually advocate the abandonment of the human adventure, and bid us content ourselves with the kind of happiness we may share with animals.[1] But we must be men, and to be a man is to be a creature which knows that it must die. We may face it philosophically and refuse to be obsessed by it, or we may refuse to face it, and throw ourselves into feverish preoccupation and forget it. This is folly. If death has the last word, life is both tragedy and farce, and we must recognise the fact. Quite so, says the humanist, but why should not reality be unpleasant and hostile? It may be, and if it is, and if the rationalist regards this as a scientific probability, then it is childish to entertain the idea of a condition of general happiness being established

[1] Cf. Mr L. T. Powys on "Natural Happiness", in the *R.P.A. Annual*, 1933.

on earth which will justify the whole process of
civilisation. On the rationalist hypothesis, the very
idea of progress is a mockery. To accept the idea
of progress as Bury defines it is indeed an act of
faith but not of saving faith. In these ultimate
issues we stultify ourselves if we believe too little.
To believe too little means that we lose the robust-
ness of rationalism without gaining the strength of
faith.

The idea of progress with which we are now
concerned can be shown to be illusory in other
ways. I need not dwell on the suspicion that the
condition of general happiness envisaged and
desired means nothing more than substantial
material comforts for all. Disraeli deservedly pil-
loried the mid-Victorian middle-class for their
confused identification of progress in civilisation
with increase in comfort. We need not, however,
through craven fear of being mid-Victorian, despise
the increase in the satisfaction of our many needs
through advancing control over nature, and yet if
the issue of the earth's business should be nothing
more than a state of society from which all unnecessary and preventable physical pain had been
eliminated, it would not suffice to justify the whole
process of civilisation. That climax would not of
itself guarantee general happiness, and there is no
reason to suppose that such an age of assured com-

fort would be intrinsically and on the whole nobler and better than all previous ages. But it is more important to note that the whole conception of value confined to some last stage or realised only in some last stage of civilisation is illusory. Theoretically, the assumption is that stage Z is supremely happy and worth while, and that stages A to Y have value not in themselves but only as leading up to Z. This concept is intolerable and untrue. Each stage must have value in and for itself, and not simply as a transition to something else. Ranke was right when he said, "Each epoch has an immediate relation to God, is not merely means and transition to something other, but is something distinct and living in itself". For persons as well as epochs, this truth is stated most forcibly, indeed is overstated in a passage from Mr Edward Thompson's account of the campaign in Mesopotamia, in his book *These Men Thy Friends*. "While the things on which historians fix their eyes are of small importance, are merely part of the wide shifting illusion that we call time, what is of importance is the tiny part that belongs to each man and each woman. It mattered nothing...that Xenophon had held a torch to Alexander's path of blood. But it did matter that Xenophon himself, whatever weariness of mind or body fell to his lot, never lost his watchful centre of spirit, but remained alert

13-2

and eager."[1] Here in my judgment Mr Thompson is too contemptuous of time, perhaps too much under the influence of Hindu ways of thinking. The things on which historians fix their eyes, when they are estimating what I might call the transitional benefit conferred by given events, are not of small importance. It did matter and does matter profoundly that the discovery of the rottenness of Persia by Xenophon and his ten thousand Greeks blazed a trail for Alexander. But Mr Thompson is right when he reminds us that the Anabasis and Xenophon's part in it are of value not merely or mainly as opening the way for Alexander. The still more important thing is the way Xenophon kept his end up, played his part:

How of the field's fortune? That concerned our leader;
Led, we struck our stroke, nor cared for doings left or
    right.
Each as on his sole head, failer or succeeder,
Lay the blame or lit the praise: no care for cowards,
    Fight.

The field and the field's fortune are not of small importance, but there is an intrinsic worth in the individual's character and action which is not dependent on or determined by the issue of the conflict. Sooner or later we must recognise with Troeltsch that "not the final stage of mankind on

[1] *Op. cit.* p. 276.

earth but the death of the individual is the limit of all philosophy of history".[1] It seems to me that Troeltsch is also right when he says that ideas like Mankind or Humanity, and Progress cannot be put into finally valid shape. "As to progress, a development of mankind as a whole no one in truth knows even from afar, and consequently no one knows any law of this development. The golden age of achieved and completed progress can comfort the modern thinker as little as the Messianic age the ancient Jews. And contrariwise the prospect of a decline, on the analogy of organic life, cannot daunt us. The last man roasting the last potato on the last coal cannot frighten us, since he has appeared on the scene several times already. When we suffer under bondage to littleness, vulgarity, confusion, and sensuality, it is still more reasonable to think of a perfecting of the individual who is capable thereof and marked out for it, beyond the death of the body than to calm one's self with an outcome of development which the last generation will enjoy and which even for them is not very probable."[2] The idea of the Progress of Humanity is not really on the same level as the ideas of Providence or personal immortality. The latter may not be susceptible of proof. The former can be shown to be illusory and unsatisfying.

[1] *Historismus*, p. 199.　　　　[2] *Op. cit.* p. 188.

I am well aware that the position I am advocating finds no favour with the modern intelligentsia in this country. Faith in a life beyond this, they constantly assure us, has been generated by primitive superstition and finds no support in science. To merge one's self in the group is the essence of religion, and the craving for personal immortality is the incidental outcome of the segregation of the individual, the sign and proof of a morbid self-consciousness. By this faith the acquisitiveness of the West extends its claims to another world. The very desire to live beyond the death of the body is a form of spiritual imperialism. To become completely disinterested, to deny ourselves finally, we must accept thoroughgoing materialism. Devotion and self-sacrifice are possible to the utmost only if one renounces all hope for one's self in another world.

Such reasoning seems at first impressive, and yet I am persuaded that it will not stand a close analysis. The psychological considerations and the anthropological observations to which it appeals can be shown to be inadequate or misinterpreted. But apart from critical analysis, this fashionable humanist outlook is incompatible with the nature of history. If the historian is concerned not simply with transitional values but, as Bertrand Russell argues, with events that have significance in themselves, intrinsic value and not merely value as links in a chain of cause and effect, then he can make nothing of his subject-matter without recognising values that endure and that are not exhausted and used up in the process which is history. If history be regarded primarily as process, then the historian has always to reckon with super-history. Even the insistence of Creighton against Lord Acton, that each age or epoch must be judged and understood first of all in accordance with its own standards, implies that each age or epoch has a distinct interest and quality of its own. But much more important is the consideration that great men can never be understood by any merely relative standards. The analysis of their time and circumstances never exhaustively explains their significance. The records of their achievements must bear the legend, "They were not of an age, but for all time", and one comes to suspect that even that proud claim is an example of litotes or meiosis. We are saying less than we mean and less than we ought. The expression 'for all time' should read 'for eternity'.

As we have already seen, the significance of each individual life cannot be estimated by its contribution to a process of development. On a war memorial in Hawarden by a curious incongruity the sentences "Some there be that have no memorial", and "their name liveth for evermore" are associated: but the paradox is a true one. Unknown to history in the narrow sense of the term, the decisions of nameless men and women are still eternally significant, their characters of permanent worth. "If there is any valid argument for a life beyond this one, it is the coherence that is built by character." The force of the argument lies in the unexhausted value and power of such a coherent character.

If history were merely the continuation of a biological process, the individual could have no significance except as a link between generations. But to try to interpret history on purely biological principles is to betray history as a science, and to adopt an indefensible scientific method. The recognition of a more abiding significance in the individual person is forced upon the historian by the very nature of his subject-matter. The disinterestedness of thoroughgoing materialism will be found to be less noble than it seemed at first sight. It is not the future of our petty selves which is at stake, but the significance of personality and so of all the distinctive qualities and values of human life. The disinterestedness commended to us will turn out to resemble the disinterestedness of the woman in the case before Solomon, who was prepared to have the child divided. Disinterestedness may be a fine moral quality, it may also be heartless brutality. The disinterestedness of materialism must inevitably degenerate into the latter. It degrades us to the level of the brute, and denies our true spiritual nature. There is in us men and women that which cannot find ultimate satisfaction in any this-world aims and hopes, and the source of our discontent is not blind selfish egotism. The fine passage on this subject in Harnack's *What is Christianity?* seems to me to have lost none of its truth. "Labour is a valuable safety-valve and useful in keeping off greater ills, but it is not in itself our absolute good, and we cannot include it amongst our ideals. The same may be said of the progress of civilisation. It is of course to be welcomed: but...it is only for a moment that it seems as if something new were coming and a man were being really relieved of his burden. Gentlemen, when a man grows older and sees more deeply into life, he does not find, if he possesses any inner world at all, that he is advanced by the eternal march of events, by 'the progress of civilisation'. Nay, he feels himself, rather, where he was before, and forced to seek the sources of strength which his forefathers also sought. He is forced to make himself a native of the kingdom of God, the kingdom of the Eternal, the kingdom of Love: and he comes to understand that it was only of this kingdom that Jesus Christ desired to speak and to testify, and he is grateful to him for it."[1]

You may say, this is the religion neither of time nor of eternity, but of old age. I do not doubt that youth must be concerned primarily with this-world objectives, with the tasks entrusted to us here and now, but it is not the decay of physical power and consequent loss of interest in this-world aims which accounts for the religious outlook of old age. It would be strange and sad if the advance of years did not bring a deeper insight into our real needs, our true position, and a more convincing awareness of eternal realities.

History, then, is more than the record of progress, but it is the record of progress, or at least the record of a process or of processes which in their sequence and development possess value. There are, it seems to me, what might be termed dramatic or romantic values in history, processes of development in which each stage may indeed have its own significance, but in which the sequence and interaction of each stage counts, and not merely the climax but the whole story has abiding interest and value. It may seem premature to speak of 'the story of mankind', though, as Bury reminds us, Christianity is committed to faith both in the unity of history and the unity of mankind,

[1] *Op. cit.* pp. 130–1.

finding the centre of interest of the story in certain events in Palestine, a shadowed cross and an empty tomb, and discovering the oneness of mankind in the fact that all men are concerned in these events. From this standpoint, the issue of earth's business, is the revelation of the sons of God, the achievement of spiritual liberty. For Dr McKerrow has insisted rightly that to make freedom the essential theme of history we must transpose it into the highest key. "Some historians make the development of 'freedom', in the secular sense, the motif of history, and they need only reinterpret the word in St Paul's sense to be right."[1] But if we cannot demonstrate in detail the truth of the Christian interpretation of history, and if with our present limited grasp of the realities of history, we must speak of multifarious distinct interests, processes, and stories, there remain these values inherent in events when taken in succession and in relation to one another. And once again we are confronted with the question, for whom do these values exist? For in the realm of values, the Berkeleyan principle, *Esse est percipi*, would seem to hold good. A value ceases to exist if it is not perceived. Unless there be some eternal mind for whom values exist, our sense of values would seem to be frustrate and irrational. For when we affirm

[1] *An Introduction to Pneumatology*, p. 32.

the presence of beauty in an object, or of nobility in an action, we affirm not indeed that the object or the action should continue for ever, unless we are with Peter on the Mount of Transfiguration and speaking foolishly, but that this vision of beauty or act of nobility should be remembered for ever. Something is here which we would fain rescue from the ravages of time. Memory is itself an attempt to arrest the flight of time, and all historical work would retrieve the past from oblivion and endow it with a kind of immortality. But if events are worth remembering, then that there should come a time when all memory of all happenings will be blotted out is in itself an intolerable evil. In these ultimate issues, it seems to me, only ontological arguments count, and their invalidity in formal logic matters not a jot. What is worthy of God must be true of Him, and a world with no enduring spiritual reality in it is the kind of absurdity which is simply incredible. There are credible absurdities, as Tertullian was aware, but a mechanistic material universe is not one of them.

The values with which the historian is dealing, if they are true values, exist only for spiritual beings, and can only exist eternally if there is a Spirit or Mind behind the universe. Humanity or the Life-force cannot be a substitute for Spirit or Mind. Those who reject the hope of personal immortality on scientific grounds cannot consistently believe in the immortality of the human race or of the life-force. As we have already recalled, the same scientific grounds forbid faith in the indefinite continuance of men and indeed of life on earth. Believers in the life-force are simple idolaters if they confine their conception of the life-force to the evidence derived from biology. They are worshipping something less than themselves in every respect except sheer vitality. If they attribute to the life-force higher qualities without scientific warrant they are really crypto-theists, either too ignorant to recognise or too proud to confess their true faith. It seems to me that only on a theistic view of the universe has history its true significance.[1]

Perhaps I should add one further comment on the philosophies which accept the second law of thermo-dynamics as ultimate, and build on this sure foundation of despair. The classic expressions of such an attitude are W. E. Henley's *Invictus* and Mr Bertrand Russell's *Free Man's Worship*. This type of rationalism is deservedly critical of all optimistic religions of life which profess to accept the same premisses. But when Mr J. C. Powys advises us to defy, to forget, and to enjoy the world there is obviously something wrong with the advice.

[1] See Note F at the end of the chapter.

To defy, you must remember; to enjoy, you must forget. Will not defiance and enjoyment alike be hollow and theatrical? Instead of wasting our lives in performing this very difficult intellectual and emotional balancing feat, why should we not recognise that the fact that the world of the physicist is apparently running down, is indeed fatal to all religions of time but leaves unimpaired the religion of eternity?

If we ignore or deny the realm of the unseen and eternal, if we treat the seen and temporal as ultimate, we must acknowledge the reign of death. The last word lies with death, and those who believe in life, progress, humanity, are fostering illusions and warming themselves at dying fires. If with Bertrand Russell and others we accept the reign of death, and assume that the process in which we are involved had a beginning and must have an end, begins in chaos and ends in darkness, starts from nothing and passes into nothingness, if we pretend to believe all this, the very animal faith which compels us to go on living gives the lie to our perverse philosophy. We can only enjoy, so long as we forget or so long as for the moment we adopt an alternative standpoint. I gather that Mr I. A. Richards can enjoy, say, the poetry of George Herbert, by adopting an 'as if' philosophy, by assuming temporarily the position of a believer. In the end, if you once commit the fallacy of treating physics as metaphysics, all your aesthetic satisfactions are illicit and contraband, secured at the price of intellectual dishonesty. But the animal faith which compels every humanist and rationalist to flout or forget his professed creed, can only be justified if it advances from the seen to the unseen, from the temporal to the eternal, from humanity to God.[1]

On the other hand, to recognise the reality of the world of eternal values, and to treat time as illusory, is likewise unsatisfying. No form of mysticism or idealism which is simply indifferent to history can give us the true interpretation of the world and of human life. We can neither treat time as equivalent to eternity nor simply hold the temporal and the eternal apart and distinct from one another.

There must be some intimate interconnection between Spirit and Matter, between the eternal and the temporal. Even Plato's illuminating description of time as the moving image of eternity does not perhaps give us quite all we need to affirm of the relation of time to eternity. It contains no doubt the profound suggestion that a whole apprehended as such in the simultaneity which is eternity may be translated into the form of tem-

[1] For a discriminating analysis of the irrational position into which Mr Richards is betrayed by his rationalism, see an article on "Poetry and Truth" by Helen Wodehouse, in *Philosophy*, October 1933.

poral succession. But we would fain discover
something more, an interplay of the eternal and
the temporal as intimate as the association and
interaction of mind and body in a psycho-physical
organism. Paradoxical and absurd as the assertion
may seem to be, the temporal process, if it be in
any degree real, must make some difference to
eternity. Apart from that which is eternal, the
world of time has no ultimate significance, but
none-the-less events in time must affect that world
of eternal values. We are in the position of Plato
when he found himself confronted with the choice
between Being and Becoming. Our only wisdom
in face of such a dilemma is to become like children
and insist on having both. Professor Whitehead
in his *Adventures of Ideas* has hazarded the prophecy,
that "that religion will conquer which can render
clear to popular understanding *some eternal greatness
incarnate in the passage of temporal fact*" (italics mine).[1]
This I believe Christianity can do and has done.
This is the essential point of the Christian's conviction that the historic Jesus and the eternal
Christ are inseparable. Gerhard Kittel thus characterises what he calls 'the scandal of particularity'
which is found at the heart of Christianity. "The
Jesus of history is valueless and unintelligible unless He be experienced and confessed by faith as

[1] *Op. cit.* p. 41.

the living Christ. But if we would be true to the New Testament we must at once reverse this judgment. The Christ of faith has no existence, is mere noise and smoke, apart from the reality of the Jesus of history."[1]

This intimate connection of temporal event with eternal realities would seem to underlie the great tradition in English poetry. It has been suggested that "the power of our poetry has been built up out of a certain strange incapacity in our poets to distinguish this world from the next".[2] They perpetually link heaven with earth, and confuse the temporal with the eternal. They are constantly disturbed like Henry Vaughan by "bright shoots of everlastingness", or they discover with Lowell that

> The real doth not clip the poet's wings,—
> To win the secret of a weed's plain heart
> Reveals some clue to spiritual things,
> And stumbling guess becomes firm-footed art.

The secret of the great tradition in English poetry from Chaucer to Robert Bridges lies in the fact that our poets have been nurtured in the Christian faith and have learnt thereby to find some eternal greatness incarnate in the passage of temporal fact.

I am not contending that all great poetry is of Christian inspiration or that all the great qualities

[1] *Mysterium Christi*, p. 49.
[2] Basil de Selincourt, *The Observer*, Nov. 12, 1933.

of English poetry must be traced to this source. But if it be true that our English poets in general are marked by their incapacity to distinguish heaven from earth, and that something of the genius of our poetry depends on this incapacity, this characteristic is Christian in origin. It derives from the fact that, as Dr Forsyth would say, Christ is seated on Parnassus.

A particular example may serve to throw into relief the nature of the more direct influence of the fundamental Christian faith. In his anthology, *The Spirit of Man*, Robert Bridges prints in succession a fine passage from the Persian mystic, Jelal-ud-din, and George Herbert's 'Hymn to Love' (Nos. 55, 56). The parallel and the contrast are alike of interest. Both describe ultimate happiness under the symbol of a feast. Both affirm the same qualifications, particularly the need of pure eyes, as essential to participation in the highest bliss. The difference between them is that the Persian mystic claims to have fulfilled the conditions, while the Christian hesitatingly accepts an invitation of which he knows he is unworthy. The first corresponds to Dr Deissmann's 'acting' mystic, who takes the initiative and seeks the eternal beyond time. For him, the Aristotelian conception of God as the unmoved mover may suffice. But George Herbert is the reacting mystic, the man

who knows that in the realm of love God is before-
hand with us, and for him the starting-point of
faith and hope and love is some insurgence of the
eternal into the field of time. Some historical hap-
pening prompts George Herbert's hymn. And its
appeal and our response to it do not depend on
any of Mr Empson's Types of Ambiguity. The
secret of the poem, of its grace and its power, is
given in the simple but striking sentence with
which Miss Helen Waddell approaches Peter Abelard's understanding of the Atonement. "We think
God is like that for ever, because it happened once,
with Christ."[1]

If the debt of poetry to Christ be undeniable,
the appeal of Christ on the wider levels of popular
understanding is still more evident. In the realms of
worship and religious experience hymnology bears
witness to the creative power of faith in the historic
Jesus as Son of God. The essence of the Christian
contention is given in a verse from a children's
hymn which may not be particularly appropriate
to children and yet contains a profound truth.
The verse describes the song for little children as

> A song that even angels
>   Can never never sing:
> They know not Christ as Saviour
>   But worship Him as King.

[1] *Peter Abelard*, p. 290.

That knowledge of Christ as Saviour, which distinguishes us from the angels, comes to us in history and can only come to us in history. It begins in time, and it issues in eternity. The same essential truth may be approached along the line of the French saying, "Souffrir passe: avoir souffert ne passe jamais". Deissmann has drawn attention to the fact that in the phrase 'Christ crucified' the participle is the perfect passive, not the aorist. σταυρωθείς would mean, 'who was once crucified', something past and done with: ἐσταυρωμένος means, 'who has been crucified and who bears the marks of his suffering still upon him'. "Suffering passes, but to have suffered passes never." "He showed them his hands and his side. Then were the disciples glad, when they saw the Lord."

The title of this closing lecture is borrowed from the masterly study of the theme by Philip Wicksteed. In his paper, he suggested that the renewed interest in the Middle Ages meant among other things a realisation of the place of fruition, of enjoyment, of the beatific vision, as the aim and heart of true religion. We have lost sight of the Church triumphant in preoccupation with the problems of the Church militant. Yet the Church militant is in the last resort a great preparative to the Church triumphant, and in love and devotion we sometimes glimpse the nature of eternal joys. The actual experiences of ecstasy and vision which come to the poet and the lover, to the mystic and the devout adoring worshipper are not really timeless and yet they seem to take us beyond time and give us glimpses, foretastes of eternity. And for us Christians such experiences here and now centre supremely on the cross and the empty tomb, on the recollection, in the mystical sense of that term, of the risen Lord who is also He who has been crucified. Thus in the now little-used hymn of the mercy-seat, Arthur H. Stowell describes the experience of the true worshipper:

> There, there on eagle's wings we soar,
> And time and sense appear no more:
> There heavenly joys our spirits greet,
> And glory crowns the mercy-seat.

This vanishing or retiring of the things of time and sense is implied in Richard Hooker's description of the devout communicant in whose mind as he comes to the table of the Lord will be no other thoughts than these, "O my God, thou art true, O my soul, thou art happy!".

And those who, like the Friends, find the outward elements a hindrance rather than an aid to communion, may and will continue to discover their true centre in the passion of our Lord:

> In the cross of Christ I glory,
> Towering o'er the wrecks of Time.

NOTE F

MR MIDDLETON MURRY AND METABIOLOGY

It is possible to resist the theistic implications of history by denying that any values are eternal, and by regarding process in time as ultimate. This is apparently the view of Mr Middleton Murry. The universe is a living organism, its unity is essentially biological, the life-process produces variations to which value attaches. The world of values constitutes a metabiological sphere, but it is continuous with and dependent on the biological life-process. The process itself is, to Mr Middleton Murry's mind, thrilling, mysterious and satisfying. In spite of his parade of metabiology, his ultimate categories are clearly biological, as is manifest from his treating values as emergent variations to which we make organic response. Those values are not eternal, they are simply variations which we should like to maintain in existence for a very long time or as long as the underlying biological process permits. This philosophy, devised simply to maintain a naturalistic monism which is itself an idle prejudice, lies open to insuperable objections. It denies the true character of our highest values. Mr Middleton Murry seemingly turns his back on Keats. It is not true that "a thing of beauty is a joy for ever: Its loveliness increases; it will never Pass into nothingness". Mr Middleton Murry may indeed assert that the embodiments of value to which he makes organic response do not pass into nothingness but into the temporal phenomenal life-process which is the whole of reality. But this assumption will not save his position. All his short-lived values pass into nothingness, unless the process of which they form part be unending. Unending temporal succession is not the equivalent of eternity, and unending phenomenal process in time cannot be the ultimate reality. And in any case we have no reason to believe that the biological process in which values inhere is unending. A thrilling mysterious process which must come to an end cannot be satisfying. It is moreover certain that no biological process embraces the universe. The concept of the universe as living organism is no more ultimate than the concept of the universe as a huge mechanism, and history cannot away with either conception. To substitute the term 'metabiological' for the terms 'historical' and 'spiritual' is no advance in understanding. It is merely a perverse darkening of counsel, a refusal to face the actual complexity of human experience.

INDEX

For EU product safety concerns, contact us at Calle de José Abascal, 56–1°, 28003 Madrid, Spain or eugpsr@cambridge.org.